Root and Blossom

By the same author

English for Diversity
Autobiography in Education
The Black Rainbow
a symposium on the state of contemporary culture
English Broadsheets
(*sets of illustrated folders*)
Introductory Series
First Series
Second Series

Approaches
(*anthologies for adolescents*)
Into Action
Our World
Asking Questions
Creating for Ourselves

Stories for Today
(*for adolescents with reading difficulties*)
Ron's Fight
Ginger and Sharon
Frank's Fire
Linda's Journey
Joe and Carol
Diane's Sister
The Big Game
Rescue at Night
June's Work

Edited by Peter Abbs
Tract
(*a quarterly journal*)
Gryphon Press, Brechfa, Llanon, Dyfed

Root and Blossom

*Essays on the Philosophy, Practice
and Politics of English Teaching*

PETER ABBS

HEINEMANN EDUCATIONAL BOOKS
LONDON

Heinemann Educational Books Ltd
LONDON EDINBURGH MELBOURNE AUCKLAND
TORONTO HONG KONG SINGAPORE
KUALA LUMPUR IBADAN NAIROBI
JOHANNESBURG LUSAKA NEW DELHI

ISBN 0 435 18028 2

Published by
Heinemann Educational Books Ltd
48 Charles Street, London W1X 8AH
Set in 11/12 Baskerville by
Malvern Typesetting Services Ltd
and printed in Great Britain by
Fletcher & Son Ltd, Norwich

Contents

for Annabel

It seems to me that we can also say of . . . institutions that they have ceased to live when they show themselves incapable of carrying on a poetry of human relations—that is, the call of each individual freedom to all the others.

Merleau-Ponty

Man is indispensable for the completion of creation; he himself is the second creator of the world, who alone has given to the world its objective existence.

Carl Jung

Introduction

The aim of this book is simple. It seeks to reassert, in a time of confusion, the value of English teaching as an aesthetic and imaginative discipline. It aims to show how English — and all the various studies and activities now connected with English in the primary and secondary schools, in the Education Departments and Colleges of Education — works, often quite unconsciously, in the intellectual framework created by the Romantic and the Existentialist movements. The book, then, is not primarily attempting to provide new subject matter so much as to forge fresh connections between the various disciplines and traditions of subjective enquiry and in so doing to provide the teacher and the student of English with a more finely detailed, a more sensitive and useful map.

I have divided the book into three parts, philosophy, practice and politics but these divisions, while never arbitrary, must not be understood as being hard and sharp. Rather, they form the different facets of the one object. We need, quite clearly, to establish both formative principles and thoroughly practical approaches. Any divorce in these matters brings distortion and disaster to both sides. At the moment, in a technological age, we are somewhat obsessed by techniques and naïvely overlook the fact that without philosophy we cannot know what ends to bend our techniques and materials to. For this reason I begin with philosophy, continue by looking at practice and end with politics. Judged not on the parts but as unity, I hope the book achieves the proper balance, the true marriage.

I would like finally to thank the following for kindly helping, in one form or another, with the writing of this book: David Holbrook, Marjorie Hourd, Kenyon Calthrop, John Morris and John Richardson. I must also thank Mrs Phyllis Wells for typing the manuscript so well and conscientiously.

PETER ABBS

Acknowledgements

Parts of this book have previously appeared in *The Use of English,
Times Educational Supplement, The Ecologist, Tract* and *Poetry
Wales.*

Chapter 7 has been previously published as the introduction to
Autobiography in Education.

Some of the poems quoted in Chapters 1 and 3 have previously appeared
in the *Poetry Festival Pamphlet* 1973, sponsored by the Herefordshire
Branch of NATE. Others have appeared in the pamphlet, *Man, Birds,
Beasts and Insects* produced by Mrs Lewis's I.L. (1974) of the Welsh
School, Ysgol Penweddig, Aberystwyth.

PART I

Philosophy

ONE

The Philosophy of English Teaching

The assumption that the more richly and energetically the human spirit builds its languages and symbolisms the nearer it comes to its ultimate being and reality [is] the idealistic minimum necessary for an adequate theory of symbolism.

P. Urban

I

In this opening essay I wish to outline and defend those powerful values and assumptions which inform the current practice of English teaching. I believe this has become an important task, for when mechanical and bureaucratical changes are ceaselessly breaking the delicate threads of continuity in education, only those imaginative disciplines, capable of boldly expressing their premises, will stand any chance of surviving. If the aesthetic disciplines, English, Drama, Art, Music, Dance, fail to provide an encompassing framework for their activities, they will perish. They will either disappear from the syllabus or, if not disappear, be amalgamated into 'Social Studies', 'Project Work', 'Liberal Studies', 'General Humanities', in such a way that they may be forced to discard all that is most intrinsic to them. English teachers, for example, may find themselves reading novels to their classes not for their essential worth as creative artefacts but for their sociological content, for their relationship, say, to the most recent statistics on abortion, crime and delinquency. They may find themselves reading Hopkins and Wordsworth not for the vision that each poet embodies in his work but for their vague bearings on the theme of pollution and industrialization. Thus expression will give way to knowledge, individual meanings to social significances. Art and literature will be ransacked[1] but

[1] In a recent series of Integrated Theme Books, for example, Shakespeare's song 'When icicles hang by the wall' is followed by the comment, 'It seems that weather conditions have not changed much since Shakespeare's time'. Dürer's drawing of a hare serves as an example of an animal which loses its coat in winter. In such a manner, the truths of imagination and sensibility are discarded for the truths of empirical science.

seldom understood. And the development of vision in the child through the powers of imagination and mimesis—the development made possible by such seminal books as Herbert Read's *Education Through Art*, Marjorie Hourd's *The Education of the Poetic Spirit*, David Holbrook's *English for the Rejected*—will have been effectively destroyed. The revolution, which placed the creative and integrating powers of the psyche at the centre of education, will have been lost to the new functionalists and the bureaucrats.

English teaching is fast approaching a cross-roads. It could, quite easily, move in different directions, severely weakening itself through dispersion. The possible directions are not difficult to envisage. As I have already implied, there is a tendency in the secondary schools for the English teacher to be working alongside the ecologist, the historian, the sociologist, his work often being guided by the controlling assumption of the *empirical nature of learning* (an assumption quite different from the one on which imaginative disciplines rest). In many books now urging reform and liberation one notices the plea for 'a truly relevant and practical education', for 'a more realistically oriented curriculum'.[2] The emphasis is nearly always on pragmatic, socially useful knowledge. 'Relevance', now, surely, an exhausted word in educational journalism has come to denote approvingly all those activities which have an immediate connection with 'contemporary issues'. It is significant that the word as generally applied in educational discourse does *not* refer either to *historic* culture or to the *inner* self (these, presumably, have become irrelevant). It is likely, then, that a large number of English teachers will turn in the direction of Sociology, treating literature neither as a heritage of unique artefacts nor as the highest expression of the human spirit, but merely as helpful documenting evidence; and regarding the classroom as the place where the major social problems are discussed and clarified.

There are others who, often under a misapprehension about the nature and purpose of imaginative work in the classroom and unsympathetic to English as Sociology, clamour for a return to traditional securities and known procedures. They wish to retreat to a time when there were impeccable and universal standards to labour systematically towards. These teachers, given the chance, would willingly return to what is commonly understood by the

[2] I have taken these phrases from Colin and Mog Ball's *Education for a Change* (Penguin) described, characteristically, on the cover as a book for 'the consumers of education'.

phrase 'an academic approach'. If a graded and comprehensive Linguistics course were to appear they would welcome it with open arms. 'At last!' they would sigh, 'an end to all this uncertainty'. Their desire for order is related dialectically to the confusion that actually does exist in many classrooms today. It must also be admitted that the concept of creativity has become largely debased, it has been used to cover a multitude of failings and to represent qualities the opposite of those it was intended to denote. As I will argue more fully later, creativity cannot be developed without the notions of form, structure, discipline and tradition. The development of creativity depends on the gradual mastering of tools and techniques in relationship to actual experience: this is true as much for the child as the living artist. Aesthetic education, if it is to be real, must be stringent, exacting, purposeful, disciplined. It must go beyond 'release' and 'therapy'—though, at the beginning, these can be important elements. As Herbert Read and Marion Richardson both pointed out, this has not always been understood. In some cases creativity has been abused by being allied with a vague permissiveness, with the notion that whatever happens in the classroom should be allowed to happen without the constraints of moral, critical or imaginative judgements. In other cases, teachers, with a primitive conception of inspiration, have urged children to write spontaneously but without alert concentration, without care for the medium or without consideration of an attentive audience. This may, of course, be a way of beginning—but if imaginative work stays at this level it will quickly deteriorate into mass cliché and private rhetoric.[3]

These comments bring us to another possible departure in English teaching: a turning towards a generously tolerant but completely mindless acceptance of whatever the pupils want to do: a sort of tepid deschooling movement *within the school.* According to this view, a teacher is there not to direct, influence or initiate but to provide the conditions the children want for their variously chosen activities.[4] The teacher as casual co-ordinator. Thus I have heard of classrooms where the children

[3] The Newsom Report complained: 'Occasionally free composition produces a shapeless mess . . . There is little pleasure or respect or skill'. See, also, Section 2 of this book for fuller discussion of these issues.

[4] These teachers often see Summerhill as the ideal school—but Summerhill lacks any awareness of the importance of aesthetic development in education. Summerhill would seem a good place for certain forms of *therapy*—but does it provide the context for the full *education* of man?

decide if they wish to work to the background blare of *Radio 1*.
And there are many classrooms in which English teaching
deteriorates to a passive cutting out of pop stars, football heroes,
cars and glossy advertisements, under the name of *Project Work*.
This can easily happen against the teacher's intentions, for it is
extremely difficult in our commercial culture to introduce critical
terms to adolescents who are powerfully bewitched by the manic
images cast by the mass-media. But I am referring to that group
of English teachers who *do not even see a problem,* who, on the
grounds of cultural relativity, see no important differences
between Beethoven and the Beatles, between *Scrutiny* and *Oz,*
between advertising and art, between television and folk culture,
and who, therefore, lacking any fundamental aesthetic and
critical principles, allow the children to decide whatever it is they
wish to do.

I have said that teachers, allowing the children to follow on
their own terms any pursuit, are taking a direction. But, of
course, such a position, leaving the child's own potential
untouched and leaving him the victim of his own commercially
exploited environment, forms not so much a coherent departure
as a failure of action, a refusal to be committed to any purposes, a
neurotic evasion. Under the mask of liberation it conceals a
steady sinking into the mire. Without doubt, those who cry out for
precise standards and those who call out for ever vaguer freedoms
are screaming at each other. They are caught, more often than
not, in a destructive dialectical relationship. So intense, so
vehement, are the feelings engendered that the real problems of
education — What are we educating a person towards? And how
do we, in as much as we are responsive and responsible teachers,
achieve it? — are evaded.

Yet in any fundamental educational discourse these large
questions must be confronted, however uncertain our manner,
however imprecise our 'answers' may seem. Aristotle remarked:

> It is the mark of the educated man and a proof of his culture that in
> every subject he looks for only so much precision as its nature
> permits.[5]

Our age, demented in its pursuit for exact knowledge (having lost
the harmony of true culture), is prone to raise only those questions
which can be given a comparatively quick mathematical or
verifiable answer. In education the questions have become

---

[5] Aristotle, *Ethics.*

predominantly administrative, quantitative and pragmatic. So, at the very moment when meanings and purposes have dwindled in our society, education has everywhere expanded into an ever greater and ever more obscure darkness. As English teachers, preoccupied with the great questions tossed into consciousness by literature, by, say, the dark sonnets of Hopkins, *Women in Love* and *The Four Quartets*, we are in an excellent position to question the present and alarming deviation from Being (towards Having), from Adequate Knowledge (towards Precise Knowledge), from Existential Truth (towards Abstract Truth). I will return to this theme later in the book; the questions that concern me here, however, are more specifically related to the actual discipline of English teaching. I hope to be able to answer them with as much precision as our discipline allows, *but no more*.

If English teaching is threatened by the ceaseless implementation of external change, if it is threatened by a sociological emphasis on facts and figures, if English teaching is, also, approaching that critical point where it could divide and weaken its energies, what preparations, what defences, what attacks, what renewals should we be making? To begin to answer these practical and political questions we must, as I have already insisted, inspect the foundations on which current day-to-day practice of English in most classrooms is built. What, as English teachers — and in asking this question I am assuming that there still is a main body of English teaching to which one can still refer — is our view of language? Of creativity? Of imagination? And, moving out more widely, of society and culture? In brief, what is our philosophy of English teaching? If we can find answers to these questions, not answers that conform to the requirements of the computer or the empirical sciences, but answers that come out of our own experience in the classroom and in the tutorial, clarifying what it is we do there, then we have unearthed those very principles from which any worthwhile future developments, whether practical or political, must spring.

II

The English teacher, it is often said, has two main obligations: he must develop in every child, as far as possible, the skills of oracy and literacy. The first responsibility of the English teacher, according to this view, is to nurture the powers of reading, writing and speaking. This, of course, is, to a large extent, the traditional notion of what English teaching should be concerned with. In, for example, *A Handbook of Suggestions for Teachers*[6] (published in 1929), the main requirements of the subject were listed as follows:

(a) *Training in speech* — To secure distinct articulation and correct pronunciation, also ability to talk English, i.e. to make statements and express thoughts and feelings clearly and correctly in speech and to listen to and understand spoken English.

(b) *Training in Reading* — To secure ability to derive from books a full measure of what they have to give of information and enjoyment, also ability to read aloud in such a way as to command attention and give pleasure.

(c) *Training in Writing* — To secure lucidity, accuracy and fitness in written statement and expression.

But such a summary, which, expressed in a more casual style is still often heard, excludes all the vital *qualitative* issues which occupy the centre of English teaching. The summary is not so much false — for, *of course,* we must develop language skills — as shallow and evasive. It is not only the skills that matter, but the many purposes to which they may be put. If we teach children to write, then *what* they write is what worries or delights, annoys or depresses us. If we teach our young to read, *what* they read, not just in the classroom but also in their own leisure time, becomes our major concern. When over 60 per cent of our literate nation read, with avidity, such gutter publications as the *Sun* and the *Express,* and, during adolescence, such books as *Chopper* and *Skinhead,* such drivel as *Jackie* and *Trend,* then I do not believe that many teachers feel that, *although they have developed a form of literacy,* they have achieved their aims. Indeed, a growing number of English teachers feel that their teaching has been turned against them, that they have nurtured skills only to multiply the assault of slogans on the child's mind. As Thomas Merriam has put it:

Having created universal literacy, the next task of education is to counter the forces which would make the literate more ignorant than the illiterate by virtue of their acquired susceptibility.[7]

I wish to return in later essays to this division, this widening gap between the ideals of true education and the realities of commercial society, but here I am anxious to register a simple but crucial point. The mere fact that a person can read and write

---

[6] *A Handbook of Suggestions for Teachers* (HMSO).
[7] Thomas Merriam, 'The Consumer Society, Education and Survival' in *Tract 10.*

does not make him educated. *English teaching cannot be adequately described in the neutral terms of the two functions of literacy and oracy.* It cannot be defined solely in terms of measurable abilities or technical achievements for English teachers find themselves equally concerned with how techniques are handled, the use to which they are put and the degree to which they inhibit or express, thwart or fulfil, the individual personality of each child. Daily and inexorably the English teacher finds himself involved with all those pressing, though often strangely elusive questions, which characterize our deeper humanity: such questions as 'Who am I?', 'What do I live by?', 'How should I live?' These, of course, are the perennial questions raised by significant literature, but they are also the questions thrown up, again and again, in children's imaginative writing, now such an important part of English teaching.

Sometimes, and particularly in later adolescence, the questions are explored in an open and stark fashion as, for example, in the following poem courageously grappling with existential meanings:

Is Man the Ruler

Is life worth living?
In this world a life is only a second
A moment snatched
Yet a creation.
Man cannot create any life except himself, yet
Because he is himself
He can only create what he already is.
Is life worth living?
Yes!
Then why in the world's existence is it so insignificant?
Anyone's life is no time
And nothing to the world
But if there was no life
There would be no world.
Man can create man
but he cannot exist on his own —
But the perfect creation after — extinction?

(JUDY BOULTON, *Sixth Form, final copy*)

Sometimes, and often around the ages of twelve and thirteen, the problem of 'Who am I?' takes a more dramatic and defiant form. In the following poem a shy and introverted child explores aggressively the potential for assertion he feels growing within himself:

His Eye's: like Black Paches
With a Whole in the Middle
the Panda tells me,:-
I know that Im not big,
but Wait. Just Wait

I know I have only, two legs and two armes
but I Will have many
When I grow,
1 Will concer, I am Maight and bold
but Wait. Just Wait.

I sit in the corner
unhappy in a zoo
thay took away My Freedom
and thats a bad thing to do
but Wait. Just Wait.

(PHILIP JOHN REES, *First Form, unrevised first copy*)

The desire for potent existence proclaimed in this poem relates to
the dread of being confined that, through the symbolism of the
bird and the cage, is expressed in the following poem by an
adolescent girl:

Caged

Today was different
Somehow.
He could not understand
His new surroundings.
Caged in, he thought,
The worst punishment
For anything so small and wild
To bear.

He missed his liberty,
The free flight he had
To see the world from
Aerial view.
Now caged, he had lost all this
And he must see the
World through
Bars of cold, hard iron,
There will be no more free flight
Anymore.

(HELENA THOMAS, *Fourth Form, final copy*)

Often, however, the workings of the imagination in the quest of
identity are infinitely more complex and suggestive than the
poems I have just quoted. Here, for example, is a densely
concentrated poem by a 'backward learner' in a secondary school
revealing an obsession with the sharp conflict between life and
death, Being and Non-Being:

Silence Broken

The trees stood like skeletons in a woody web.
I looked up and saw a nest of wood decayed and dead.
I saw a bird which disappeared into the twisted den.
Then I heard a shot which would have shattered any man.
And the bird which flew was dead.

(BOY, Third Form, final copy)

The language has the resonance of Shakespeare ('the woody web'
has a similar sinister quality as 'rooky wood' in *Macbeth,* a play
the boy, according to his teacher, did not know). What had
released this short and powerful poem? Some primary energy, I
would suggest, within the boy, an inner force seeking to symbolize
his own fears and apprehensions about death. A close study of
children's writing would confirm, among other things, Victor
Frankl's contention that, man is 'primarily motivated by a search
for a meaning to his existence'.[8] The will to meaning and psychic
wholeness is demonstrated in poem after poem written in the
classroom.[9]

Here, then, we discover the first main premise on which much
of our work depends. *We assume that there is an innate need in
each personality to shape, to articulate, to make and symbolize
in the quest for existential understanding and fulfilment.* In
encouraging, as we do, children to write not only correctly but
also to feel, sense, probe and recreate actual experience, we are
committed to the principle that every child, in different ways and
in different degrees, is a creator; not just a receiver but also a
maker of symbols and meanings.

But this principle, indispensable as it is, yet expresses a rather
lop-sided truth for we know from our study of literature that
culture is not only the personal creation of each individual but
also the possession of a community and a nation. Every child, like
every poet or artist, may be a creator but, at the same time, he

---

[8] Victor Frankl in *Psychotherapy and Existentialism* (Penguin).
[9] See poems on pp. 77, 78, 80, 85, 96, 100 for further important examples.

depends on a particular context, which transcends him, a context which provides both his materials and the traditions within which he must struggle to convey his own particular vision of the world. This is why in the classroom the teacher will often introduce a particularly successful poem (like D. H. Lawrence's *Snake* or *Bats*) before asking the class to write. And this is why he also relates, when it seems appropriate, the children's poems to what is given in the inherited traditions (now, due to our detailed knowledge of most historic cultures, enormously wide). After reading back the poems *Panda* and *Caged,* for example, the teacher might introduce the Chinese poem *The Red Cockatoo*[10] (written in AD 820):

The Red Cockatoo

Sent as a present from Annam —
A red cockatoo.
Coloured like the peach-tree blossom,
Speaking with the speech of men.
And they did to it what is always
   done
To the learned and eloquent.
They took a cage with stout bars
And shut it up inside.

He might, also, consider showing the writers certain visual artefacts which embody the same oppressive fear: for example, Van Gogh's *Prisoners* and Zadkine's sculpture *The Prisoner*. In making such works available, at the very point when they touch upon the actual preoccupations of the class — or of certain individuals in the class — the teacher is, without forced intrusion, actually sustaining and developing the children's own quest for authenticity of Being. He is saying, as it were, 'Look, others have felt like this and have had, like you, the courage to say so. To feel like this, although it may seem strange, is, in truth, to be a living member of humanity'. Individuality and solidarity, self and others, innovation and tradition are, thus, quietly knitted together. If we are to encourage and develop creativity in the classroom and in the seminar, such confirmation is essential.

The powers to improvise and create, whether in writing or drama, art, dance or music, depend, to a degree greater than we are sometimes inclined to think, on the materials and patterns of

---

[10] By Po Chü-I translated by Arthur Waley in *170 Chinese Poems* (Constable).

interpretation given by historic culture. We can see this most clearly if we briefly consider — as Marjorie Hourd, David Holbrook and Marion Milner have constantly suggested we ought to — the *personal* origins of culture: origins which the teacher becomes slowly aware of as he observes the very different ways in which children respond to imaginative challenges in the classroom.

Culture, for the individual, begins with his play-and-feeding experiences and play-and-feeding is initiated by the mother. We know that the baby who is not played with, cuddled, dandled, smiled at, spoken to, sung to, but merely fed is so culturally starved that he loses the will to live and, in one form or another, dies. Culture, at this early stage of development, consists of *the forms* of response (particularly the mother's response but also the father's and other members of the family) which meet the baby's instinctive assertions and, most particularly, the instinctive need for food. The psychotherapist Rollo May in *Power and Innocence*[11] confirms these remarks:

> If the infant is denied the experience that his actions can get a response from those around him — as shown in Rene Spitz's studies of the pitiable infant orphans in Puerto Rico who were given no attention by nurses or other mother substitutes — the infant withdraws into a corner of his bed, does not talk or develop in other ways, and literally withers away physiologically and psychologically. The ultimate in impotence is death.

Rollo May in *Power and Innocence* is drawing attention to the power that exists within each child from the moment of birth and what happens to the child when the demands made by that power are not met. I am more anxious to draw attention to the *cultural nature of the responses* given to the powerful but yet utterly dependent infant: to the talking,[12] the singing, to the smiling and to all those physical gestures which all together convey to the child the feeling of being (at best) welcomed into the human world.

As English teachers, we work on the assumption that each child has an innate potentiality to symbolize experience, but this potentiality depends, to a large extent, on the mother for its release. It is in response to the mother that the child comes to return the smile that it has been given, the sounds that have been

[11] *Power and Innocence* (Souvenir Press).

[12] It is interesting here to ponder on the phrase 'the mother-tongue' to denote a person's first language.

lovingly sent to him, the gestures that have been freely made for
him. The child's identity develops through imitating and making
his own these formative acts of cultural exchange. Yet, even at
this early age of oral and gestural mimesis there is an essential
element of creativity, a delight in being that derives from the
power to express being, for as Martin Buber has written: 'What
the child desires is its own share in this becoming of things: it wants
to be the subject of this event of production'.[13] Here, then,
between the mother and child we are able to locate the personal
origins of cultural experience. When the infant develops an
almost obsessive attachment to a cuddly rag, a universal event in
childhood across, it would seem, all cultures, the child makes
another great stride in cultural evolution:

> Imaginative play with this first symbol helps a child towards a greater
> sense of his own secure existence—and the nature of others and the
> world. It is also his first step towards a human culture—and so his
> cuddly rag is later to join Mozart's Clarinet Quintet, *Dombey & Son*,
> the capacity to make an omelette, and King's College Chapel, as
> cultural things he has 'taken into himself' to enrich his inner
> resources.[14]

The teacher, by providing a discipline for creativity, by
extending the perspectives given by the family, by establishing a
communal context for cultural activity, by making himself
available for disinterested discussion and comment, adds to the
indivisible process of psychic growth. Where events in the family
have been predominantly destructive so that experience is riddled
with anxiety, suspicion and hate (leading in the child either to
depressive withdrawal or manic bursts of action—or both),
schooling becomes, likewise, a hazardous and difficult enterprise.
Concerned teachers working with deprived adolescents will
frequently say: 'I have come on the scene too late. Too much has
already happened. To have stood a chance, I should have been
there when the child was born.' The present disintegration of the
family portends a future with increasing crime, vandalism,
schizophrenia, a future characterized by a deep vacuity of 'inner'
experience and by extraordinary outbursts of violence, for the
most part aimless, in the 'outer' world. It is disturbing to find that
already in many of our large city schools teachers are

[13] Martin Buber, *The Writings of Martin Buber* (Meridian Books).
[14] David Holbrook in 'The Corruption of Symbolism', *Tract 10*. For a full discussion of
the location of cultural experience in infancy see Winnicot's *Playing and Reality*, the book
from which many of the above comments have been derived.

complaining about a growing number of children who seem to have become unteachable.

I hope to have briefly related the English teachers' commitment to cultural development to the personal origins of cultural experience. I want now to consider the *anthropological* origins of cultural experience — for here, too, we find much to confirm and nourish the day-to-day work in the classroom, and here, too, we discover a development in cultural and symbolic experience similar to that in the family, beginning humbly and slowly stretching out towards ever more intricate and complex patterns.

'Greek culture did not begin with the Parthenon; it began with a white-washed hut on a hillside. Culture has always developed as an infinitely slow but sure refinement and elaboration of simple things'.[15] From the first rhythmic movements of the body, instinctively seeking pattern and poise, Paleolithic man would seem to have slowly developed the abstract art of music and the power of song, first putting meaningless sounds, later meaningful words, to certain beats and sequences, thus, refining and elaborating the rhythmic patterns which previously only the body had been able to express. In the first seed of dance and movement were locked all the subsequent branches of the arts: music and poetry; art (probably first expressed in the decoration of the body); and drama. It is fascinating to note, in passing, that all these arts existed often in highly developed forms in early Neolithic societies. Over thousands of years, man slowly developed and refined the power to symbolize, the power through gestures, through patterns, through colours, through rituals, through sounds, through words,[16] *to make his experience visible to himself and to others.* Through the energy of the symbol, he could draw the external world into his consciousness where he could ponder its nature, purpose and meaning. And, perhaps, even more important, through the symbol he could give objective form to what lurked within him, he could catch and hold up for appreciation and consideration the elusive phantasies, the dark urges, the tender feelings, the mysterious voices, which streamed within him. Through the art of naming and patterning, through developing techniques for expressive articulation, primitive man was able to unify and condense the various urges that poured discordantly through him. Through the power of the symbol he

---

[15] Herbert Read in *To Hell with Culture* (Routledge & Kegan Paul).
[16] For a lucid discussion of the origin and development of sound and word see C. M. Bowra's *Primitive Song* (Mentor Paperback).

was able to become aware of parts of his nature that would otherwise have remained dangerously inchoate. Merleau Ponty has written:

> Great prose is the art of capturing a meaning which until then had never been objectified and of rendering it accessible to everyone who speaks the same language.[17]

I am suggesting that providing we interpret the word 'meaning' in a wide sense — so that it includes feeling, vision, phantasy, intuition — this is true of all the arts in their formative state. In the first signifying sound, in the first expressive gestures, in the first streak of colour transferred from nature to the human face, was an attempt to capture and enhance a meaning which, until that moment, had been inaccessible to the human race. Simple beginnings, it may be said — but, as with the child's first smile, first words, first intimate 'object', harbouring immense developments.

Over the last decade or so, such broad reflections on the nature of culture have brought us to an important re-definition of that word. As English teachers, we find ourselves using the word to denote an astonishingly varied range of activities. Certainly our understanding of the word, while incorporating Matthew Arnold's description of culture as 'the best that has been thought and known' and 'the study of perfection', goes far beyond it. We see culture as being more dynamic, more intimate (with its origins in the family) and more far-reaching. The words which Arnold habitually uses to describe culture, 'thought', 'knowledge', 'study', 'perfection', 'disinterested pursuit', all suggest an essentially intellectual direction of attention. The words also seem to exclude the great and equally important pursuits of art, music, architecture, sculpture, carving, dance, sacrament and ceremony.[18] Arnold, one feels, would not have recognized the physical beauty of a Negro carving, nor, perhaps, would he have responded to the following poems by eleven-year-old children naïvely identifying with the movements of a fox:

---

[17] Quoted in *The Prose of the World: Merleau-Ponty* (Heinemann Educational Books).

[18] An exclusion which has continued in F. R. Leavis' work and which has narrowed cultural studies giving intensity and depth but sacrificing seminal energies. For broad studies of culture we have to turn, largely, to America: to the works of Susanne Langer and Lewis Mumford.

The Fox

Snifing the ear around.
Smeling everi danger around.
Sniacing in the long gras.
Twards his feathrd prai.

Geting to the Hen hous
Lifting the doar with his noas
Geting in and snifing
Jympig at his feddare prai

Runig out with a hen
Runig runig to his den
Dogs barcin and howlin
The fox has got away.

Geting hoam starfun
His mat is waiting.
Eating, eating, eating
Tel the earli moaning

(SARAH: *aged 11, unrevised first copy*)

The Fox
I am the fox i live in a polus under the urth all the animals are a frayd
of my I wonder arawnd at nigh lick a bal of fier my fyr is licke felfe.
When I wonder a rawnd mebe ail hunt my prai and faind a hear with
fur lick sgragi old tits and tats from a Jumbl sel.

(IONA, *aged 11, unrevised first copy*)

That the children's mother-tongue was Welsh (which, of course,
accounts for the phonetic spelling of English) would have pleased
him even less, for Arnold was not truly aware of the need for
cultural diversity. In his official report of 1852 Arnold wrote:

It must always be the desire of a Government to render its
dominions, as far as possible, homogeneous . . . Sooner or later, the
difference of language between Wales and England will probably be
effaced . . . an event which is socially and politically so desirable.[19]

Politically and socially desirable? To efface a language, a unique
and ancient window on the world? To destroy a heritage? To make
culture homogeneous? These are perverted wishes for a man of

[19] Quoted by Saunders Lewis in *The Fate of the Language* (BBC 1962). For a full
discussion of the Welsh language see *Presenting Saunders Lewis* (University of Wales
Press) and also Gerald Morgan's *The Dragon's Tongue* (Christopher Davies).

culture, and we can only understand them, I suspect, by recognizing the narrowness of his definition of culture; the confining of cultural forms to the urbane, the civilized, the intellectual, the Hellenic, the Perfect. The lucidity of the rational ideal, so nobly incarnated in Greek culture, and which Arnold admired so fervently for its sweetness and light, blinded him to the need for cultural variegation. Arnold's failings here belonged to his age — an age only too ready to export its faith and culture while importing the needed raw materials for endless industrial expansion. Even that enlightened Man of Letters, Emerson, could write about the Indians, who as we now know, were the custodians of an extraordinary life-wisdom:

> Alas red men are few, red men
> are feeble.
> They are few and feeble and
> must pass away.

Today we witness a world stretching from New York to Moscow so artifical and so banal, so devoid of beauty and diversity, that the spirit calls out for the resurrection of all those cultures that have been so recently destroyed or are now in their present death-throes. In this respect T. S. Eliot in *Notes towards the Definition of Culture* is so much more profound than Arnold. T. S. Eliot in that book claimed:

> It would be no gain whatever for English culture, for the Welsh, Scots and Irish to become indistinguishable from Englishmen — what *would* happen, of course, is that we should all become indistinguishable featureless 'Britons', at a lower level of culture than that of any of the separate regions. On the contrary, it of great advantage for English culture to be constantly influenced from Scotland, Ireland and Wales.
> . . . It is an essential part of my case, that if the other cultures of the British Isles were wholly superseded by English culture, English culture would disappear too.

Although it is late in time, and, although much has been irreparably damaged, it is vital that we now attempt to establish and develop a pattern of communities and cultures which relate *not symbiotically but dialectically* to one another. I will return to this theme again in the concluding section of this book.

I am suggesting that our view of culture is both richer and deeper than Arnold's 'study of perfection'. We see culture as being created by some irrepressible energy in the individual psyche which seeks through the symbol to make patent the hidden self and the relationship of that self to others and the outside world. At the same time, we see that individual expression could not take place were it not for that body of culture which is transmitted from generation to generation through the mother, the family and the various organs of education. We see culture as manifesting itself in games, toys, clothes, cooking, customs, rituals, architecture, gardening, literature, art, carving, sculpture, playground songs, religion, dance, drama, and perhaps most deeply of all, in the language.[20] A language embodies the specific and complex response of a people to innumerable experiences over thousands of years: it thus carries with it a sort of life-wisdom.

Through all these symbols and artefacts, some inherited, others created, a sense of *I-living-in-a-world-of-relationships* is developed. The symbol integrates and gives coherence to what might otherwise be a bombardment of dizzy sensations, a chaos of disorganized impulses, an endlessly shifting kaleidoscope of impressions. Culture, in this way, comes to define both the individual and the nation.

English teachers for some time have been working, often intuitively, on such an assumption. It is then exciting to find that a number of anthropologists, questioning the conventional notion that man was primarily a tool-maker, have come to a similar conclusion. Lewis Mumford in *Art and Technics*,[21] examining the nature of man from a study of his origins, claimed:

> Man was perhaps an image-maker and a language-maker, a dreamer and an artist even before he was a tool-maker. At all events, through most of history, it was the symbol, not the tool, that pointed to his superior function.

Ernst Cassirer in *An Essay on Man*[22] claimed:

> Between the receptor system and the effector system, which are to be found in all animal species, we find in man a third link which we may describe as the *symbolic system*. This new acquisition transforms the whole of human life. As compared with the other animals man lives not merely in a broader reality: he lives, so to speak, in a new *dimension* of reality . . . Language, myth, art, and religion are parts

[20] This does not mean, of course, that these activities are all on the same level or embody the same intentions.

[21] Lewis Mumford, *Art and Technics* (Columbia University Press).

[22] Ernst Cassirer, *An Essay of Man* (Bantam Books).

of this universe. They are the varied threads which weave the symbolic net, the tangled web of human experience. All human progress in thought and experience refines upon and strengthens this net.

In the light of these observations, Ernst Cassirer suggests we should not define man in terms solely of intellect (*animal rationale*) but in terms of his fundamental power to symbolize. We should name man the *animal symbolicum*. In *Philosophy in a New Key* Susanne Langer, a student of Ernst Cassirer, declared the positive principle of her work in this way:

> I believe there is·a primary need in man, which other creatures probably do not have, and which activates all his apparently unzoological aims, his wistful fancies, his utterly impractical enthusiasms, and his awareness of a 'Beyond' filled with holiness. This basic need . . . is the need of symbolism.

For the Symbolic Philosophers man is not fully comprehended by the partial concepts of 'tool-maker' (coming from the bias of the Industrial Revolution) or 'naked ape' (coming from the bias of biology and pseudo-psychology) or 'a reflexive thinking machine' (coming from the bias of mechanistic science) for as a maker of symbols he transforms his natural state and his experience becomes, at the same time, both open and unique. In his poem *The Animals* Edwin Muir expresses the distinction of man eclipsed by these pervasive but hopelessly false definitions:

> They [the animals] do not live in the world,
> Are not in time and space.
> From birth to death hurled
> No word do they have, not one
> To plant a foot upon,
> Were never in any place.
>
> For with names the world was called
> Out of the empty air,
> With names was built and walled,
> Line and circle and square,
> Dust and emerald;
> Snatched from deceiving death
> By the articulate breath.

With man the world is given a second existence born through the imagination and the artefact.

Here, then, I contend we have the generative principles of a philosophical conception of man which clarifies what we intuitively work towards in the classrom. In the development of my argument I am aware of both digressing and of making short-cuts; I would like, therefore, to summarize the salient points of the discussion in a number of closely inter-related propositions:

1. Culture is a primary reality having both an affective and cognitive influence on human life. Culture not only cuts out the channels through which our feelings flow, it also reveals to us certain relationships and meanings in the world.

2. The need to express and shape, the need to symbolize, exists in every child.

3. Through speaking, through writing, through miming and acting, the child is able to discover and present himself both to himself and, through the teacher and the class, to society.

4. The child's creativity, however, can only be released, stimulated and developed through a subtle and continuous contact with the surrounding culture.

5. This contact begins at birth with the loving relationship between mother and baby. The teacher-child relationship is an extension and elaboration of this early encounter. (This is the deep meaning of teachers being *in loco parentis*.)

6. The success of the English teacher to develop the child's powers to innovate and to put him gently in touch with his literary heritage will partly depend on his being able to secure an enfolding atmosphere of trust and respect.

7. Skills and techniques (spelling, punctuating, paragraphing, logical thinking, etc.) are a subordinate but necessary part of creative activity. They have value not in themselves but only in terms of what they help to create or express. English teaching is an imaginative and aesthetic discipline.

These propositions, once stated, may well seem obvious enough. I hope this is the case, because I have been arguing that these are the foundations on which the activity of the English teacher rests. Yet if we compare these propositions to those that govern our present civilization we see that they hold a cause for severe discontent with our society and, also, possess a potentially revolutionary energy. We know that in our society, it is not culture, but money and technical know-how which constitute the primary reality. We know that most of the culture in our society is based not on trust and love, but on anxiety and hate, depending for its success on clever manipulation and organized seduction.

We sense here an immense conflict between the sanities of true culture and the insanities of an unbridled civilization. This conflict is beginning to create a politics of English teaching — a politics to which I will return in the concluding essays of this book — but it is important, first, that we become fully aware of the split between the philosophical assumptions of the creative English teacher (and, of course, other teachers working within the expressive and subjective disciplines) and the assumptions which inform and unify contemporary society. It is to the crisis, created by this widening gap, that I now wish to turn.

TWO

English in Crisis

Romantic melancholy was no mere matter of languor or the vapors: nor was it an outbreak of personal neurosis, impotence, or sickness among a few individuals: rather it was a revelation to modern men of the human condition into which he had fallen, a condition that is nothing less than the estrangement from Being itself.

William Barrett

It may startle many readers to suggest that English teaching is in a state of crisis. What sort of crisis is it? What has brought it about? And how can it be met? At the outset it is important to stress that the crisis I sense concerning English teaching is not an inward crisis, not an irreconcilable splitting within itself (though, as I have already argued, this is a possibility within the near future), but a crisis in relationship, more specifically, in its relationship to schools and the surrounding culture (if such a word can be legitimately used to denote that world of commercial values, images, and symbols, artificially created in capital cities and disseminated across entire countries). In fact, it is the very order which still exists in the main stream of English teaching, an order which has its roots in the tougher side of the Romantic movement and which is now finding further confirmation in the Phenomenological and Existentialist movement which has precipitated the crisis I am anxious to evoke and define.

Here it must suffice to point to the tension which exists in many schools between the direction in which the English teacher is moving and the over-all direction which is determined by the structure of the school. The English teacher is now committed to both liberating and refining the child's powers of thinking, feeling, imagining, perceiving, sensing, relating, through the medium of words and gesture (in writing, in reading, in discussing, in drama). Schools however tend to regard the child as a unit who must coincide exactly with his position in the abstract equation of the educational process. As schools become

larger, the child becomes less and less the centre of his own
education and more and more an anonymous part of the complex
machinery which surrounds him, supports him, but does not
recognize him. As schools amalgamate and as numbers steadily
increase, so is the need for bureaucracy born: for an excess of
organization, regulations, syllabuses, 'communications' and
examinations. As our schools become vast and heterogeneous, so
the authorities, in order to survive, feel impelled to foster a
homogeneity which can never be anything more than
institutional. Relationships between the teachers and pupils
deteriorate to a casual and general 'jogging along', with the result
that the overt content of the subject is made all important, while
any hidden emotional or personal meaning is rendered
superfluous. The learning process becomes crude, mechanistic,
often aggressive and, above all, meaningless. Carl Jung pointed
to these dangers when he wrote:

> The larger a community is, the more will the individual be morally
> and spiritually crushed and as a result, the one source of moral and
> spiritual progress for society is choked up. Naturally the only thing
> which can thrive in such an atmosphere is sociability and whatever is
> collective in the individual. Everything individual in him goes under,
> i.e. is doomed to repression. The individual elements lapse into the
> unconscious, where by the law of necessity, they are transformed into
> something essentially baleful, destructive and anarchical.[1]

It is a harsh comment to make, but Jung's analysis fits many of our
large city schools perfectly.

One of the many unfortunate results of this sort of casual
teaching ('containing the children' as I have heard it called)
which comes to the front in large schools, is that the pupils' tendency to see life through crude, stereotyped terms is reinforced.
Working in such schools, I invariably found that wherever I
attempted to present an 'open situation', I was greeted with such
anxious remarks as, 'We don't know what you mean, Sir', 'Write
it up and we'll copy it', 'Tell us how many words'. Young
adolescents were insisting that an open situation should be closed
immediately. Right or wrong, tick or cross, good or bad, these
were the only evaluative schemata which had been engendered.
Fundamental disagreement, where it existed, was solved either by
the power of the fist or the caustic phrase. Thus, ironically, life in
school was reduced to the level of the trash comic and the sleazy

[1] Jung, *Two Essays on Analytical Psychology*, (Routledge & Kegan Paul).

thriller: in both, communication took place through the fist, through monosyllabic grunts and through threats of imminent attack. That vivid experience of being uncertain, of being in a vast world between definite answers, of not knowing exactly but of plunging out on one's own terms — surely characteristic of genuine educational activity? — had been effectively destroyed in these children. In the darker moments of reflection, I couldn't help feeling that the combined forces of the family, the school and the commercial media had blinded and brutalized these children for life.

As schools become large, they tend to become bureaucratic, and education, following the impetus given by the passion for administration, tends to become both streamlined and superficial. In such a situation, English teaching which bases itself on a personal and enduring relationship between the teacher and the child, and which seeks, through creating an open space, a wholeness of response, becomes problematic.

I am, perhaps, here describing an obvious point of discord. But I now want to suggest that this discord echoes a much deeper and more complex discord between the philosophy which underlies English teaching and the philosophy which underlies our technocratic society. I have said that English teaching today has its roots in the more vigorous and alert side of the Romantic Movement. The Romantics, as is now well understood, asserted, against the reductive philosophy of materialism, the inward and symbolic truths of consciousness — a consciousness which was essentially subjective, and which could not, therefore, be understood through the objective categories of scientific enquiry. Without any doubt, we are still living in the dark shadow of this immense ideological conflict, although literal rationalism is still the prevailing force. Nor is this altogether surprising for it was inevitable that the very success of the scientific method in the physical sciences meant that it would be applied to probe and analyse the truths of consciousness.

Schiller in his letters *On the Aesthetic Education of Man* wrote with remarkable perspecuity:

> But at the present time material needs reign supreme and bend a degraded humanity beneath their tyrannical yoke. Utility is the great idol of our age, to which all powers are in thrall and to which all talent must pay homage. Weighed in this crude balance, the insubstantial merits of Art scarce tip the scale, and, bereft of all encouragement, she shuns the noisy market-place of our century. The

spirit of philosophical inquiry itself is wresting from the imagination one province after another, and the frontiers of art contract the more the boundaries of science expand.

The consequences of this great intellectual and practical effort to understand man rationally and scientifically have been disastrous—for, by making man an object among objects, it deprived him of a sense of personal meaning, that necessary human dimension of inwardness, when, historically, he most needed to sense his own human worth to control and limit the powerful machinery which had been created by the scientific and industrial revolution. And today we live in a world society (in as much as its patterns are dictated by the technocracies of Europe, Russia and America) which still insists on the very programme of productivity and measurement which inexorably drives us to the very edges of spiritual and biological life. Philip Sherrard, in a letter to *The Times*, defined the plight of our civilization as follows:

> We are coming face to face with the collapse of our modern industrial society and with the tragic inadequacy of the values on which it has been based.
>
> We have fabricated this society, broadly speaking, on the assumption that man is a two-legged animal whose destiny can be fulfilled through the satisfaction of his material needs. On this assumption we have directed almost our entire energies to investigating and exploiting the physical world and to gearing our labour to the production of an ever-increasing number and variety of material objects. The urban industrial world which has emerged as a result is one in which the fundamental dignity of man—his unique and absolute value as a person with an inward creative dimension which no degree of material well-being can satisfy—is virtually obliterated. *What we are witnessing now, and will witness in more dramatic forms in the years to come, is the break-up of a social order constructed on the basis of a lie.*
>
> *Urban industrialism, like other products of the age of scientific rationalism and empiricism, is the result of an experiment. It is an experiment which has failed. Its failure is evident not only in its devastation of the natural environment but also in the fact that it has exacerbated practically every evil it was meant to eliminate.* Moreover, because of its totalitarian character it has left us extremely ignorant about what to put in its place, about how to develop new forms of life and society.[2]

(My italics)

---

[2] Letter in *The Times*, 14 December 1973.

The growing realization that the experiment, set in motion by such figures as Descartes, Galileo , Kepler, Bacon, Harvey and Newton, has failed, together with the growing apprehension of imminent catastrophe, is slowly drawing together responsible individuals from many different disciplines and types of social involvement, and it forms the background against which the present crisis in English teaching must be understood.

In using this familiar metaphor of 'background' I hope I am not making the struggle seem remote and outside of everyday experience: for such a struggle takes place daily in most schools in a thousand diverse incidents. When an English teacher is questioned, as he often is, about the point of drama or discussion or creative writing (for what good will it be in later life in the consumer society?) he is being asked to face the same functional life-confining attitude which Blake and Coleridge felt they were combating. Conversely when the teacher affirms a fine movement of the body in drama, a delicate perception in writing, a sympathetic understanding in discussion, he is affirming some of those qualities of being which the Romantic revolution understood as the alternative to the essentially passive, the outwardly insatiable but inwardly stunted consciousness, created by the functional society. Such affirmation by the teacher and by the children of individual and imaginative activity is the surest way of developing that deep reservoir of creativity which the child/adolescent/adult will need if he is to retain his own humanity in the shrill and self-confessed inhumanity of modern life.

In schools the English teacher, also, finds himself confronting the values of the wider culture in the comics and magazines and paperbacks that his pupils bring in. Somehow, in the classroom and outside of it, the teacher must come to terms with them. In *The Preface to the Lyrical Ballads,* Wordsworth claimed:

> A multitude of causes, unknown in former times, are now acting with continued force to blunt the discriminating powers of the mind, and unfitting it for all voluntary exertion . . . reduce it to a state of almost savage torpor.

Today, the discriminating powers of people seem not so much to be blunted as destroyed — which, of course, from the standpoint of the consumer economy, is a fitting psychological state for man. David Holbrook in *The Masks of Hate*[3] has shown how, as the

[3] Holbrook, *The Masks of Hate* (Pergamon).

powers of alert discrimination have evaporated, so has the naked exploitation of sexuality and anxiety increased. He has also shown how pornography is an extreme expression of that literalism, that exclusive emphasis on objectivity, in which we have been imprisoned since the rise of science and which I have already referred to. Again it can be seen how, in his attitude to the more commercial aspects of the mass media, the English teacher is opposed to the prevailing assumptions underlying our civilization. In the responses and preoccupations of much of the pupils' work he will sense, again and again, the way in which their experience is vitiated by commercial propaganda. The following passages are typical examples of work from that 'submerged 60 per cent' which we haven't even begun to educate:

> Each night we go out and if we see a fight or any Hell's Angels we join in and lay the boot in which are hob-nails or lace-up shoes . . .
>
> (13-YEAR-OLD GIRL)

> I prefer skinheads without beards . . . I would like him to have short hair. No beard. I don't mind little moustaches, to be dressed in a smart brown flares with turn ups single breasted jackets. He must wear Benshires mens and above all if he doesn't where Brute I don't go for him.
>
> (14-YEAR-OLD GIRL)

> Terry went around the streets and got all his mates Rusco, Stan Hill, Butch, Robby, paul, ian they all marched down and waited outside for them. (they walked out to face them) the Withywood mob layed into them and there was fists flying round and Terry and Curry who was bleeding all over. they walked off and I left the Ashton Park mob sprawling on the floor and curry never bothered our Terry again.
>
> (13-YEAR-OLD BOY)

Such writing, revealing so dramatically the relationship between advertising, violent sex films, pulp fiction and the consciousness of the young, compels the teacher to develop, in the classroom, approaches to the critical study of the mass media and the advertising system which it is, as Fred Inglis has shown,[4] locked into. It urges him to develop, as best he can, an awareness of social exploitation, of the deliberate and continuous cor-ruption of language, symbolism and conscience. It also makes' him increasingly aware of how English teaching is flowing

---

[4] See *The Imagery of Power* (Heinemann Educational Books), a stringent study of advertising and its relationship to the 'consumer-society'. For a detailed commentary on commercial symbolism see Chapter 4 of the present book.

counter to the main current. But this is an energetic and positive counter-movement because it becomes increasingly clear that the main current is heading in a direction which threatens to destroy not only the courageous ideals and diverse artefacts of man but also life itself.

It is not surprising that in many classrooms there are children who, immersed in the main current of our culture, are confused or bewildered by what the English teacher is trying to do. Nor is it surprising to find that often the authorities of the school do not appreciate the purpose of imaginative work and even feel threatened by it. It is thus to be expected that many English teachers — particularly students, who are highly exposed to the contradictions in our educational system — experience themselves as being divided within, tossed between the pressures of the school, the pressures of modern culture and the pressures which stem from the meaning of a genuinely imaginative discipline. This sense of inner division can be seen as a further expression of the crisis in English teaching which I am seeking to clarify.

What can be done? English teachers need a supporting community, a community which is capable of confirming the exacting and yet often unappreciated work in the classroom. Departments and Colleges of Education could provide the centres for such communities (as well as create the possibilities for genuine exchanges, the privileges of the colleges being open to the teachers, and the difficulties of the schools undertaken by lecturers and educational theorists). Unfortunately many lecturers feel they have escaped from schools and are only too anxious to preserve a dignified, but necessarily deadening, isolation. On the other hand, many teachers, who are given little break from the exhausting, ceaseless demands of teaching, reject too easily any ideas or suggestions which come from the colleges. This deadlock must be broken for it dams up the very channels through which effective change might come.[5]

We need also to widen our conception of the purpose of the school. Our views are still too narrow, too functional. Instead of seeing the school as a preparation for the consumer society, we should see it as a centre for the local community, both cultural and political. The school should endeavour to embody all those alternatives to technocracy which are so insidiously suppressed by the mass media. I mean that schools should now become centres of resistance, pitting values, meanings and local rights against the

[5] For a full discussion of the changes needed in Colleges of Education see Chapters 6 and 7.

insatiable and amoral demands of Progress, Profits and
Productivity. The school should serve as a genuinely critical force
in the community. On the more positive side, the school should be
committed to transmitting to the people (as well as the children) a
whole range of art and craft forms, to recreating local life and
making possible again that sense of community without which life
becomes vague and void of purpose. These aims will be more
easily realized in the remoter parts of England, Scotland and
Wales where communities and popular art forms still exist (if not
in the present moment, at least in people's memories). They will
be more difficult to achieve in the vast twilight urban areas where
families are restricted to the choice of isolating themselves before
the entertainment machine or isolating themselves in cars to 'get
away' for a time. But, of course, this is only to say that in urban
areas the need for the schools to become real cultural centres is
desperate.

What further changes do the premises of the philosophy of
English teaching call for? What active political direction should
English teachers now take? These are difficult questions but
necessary ones for they follow naturally from the diagnosis if it is
to be found reasonably accurate. It is obvious that the direction
must be determined by English teachers as a whole who, through
discussion, through a common sharing and evaluating of
experience, come to a common sense of purpose. Such discussion
could come, as it has in America, when it may be too late, when
the grievances and frustrations have reached such an intensity
that they will not be comforted and consequently insist on taking
the absolute and violent path of destruction. It would be re-
assuring if we could discuss the acute problems raised by
education and the culture of which education is one reflection,
before that ultimate and irreversible point of crisis is reached.

There are signs that this may happen: James Britton
summarized a manifesto issued at the International Conference of
English Teachers at York 1971 as follows:

In the belief that what we already knew about English teaching was
enough to constitute a challenge to existing educational institutions,
should we not, here and now, turn our attention directly upon the
social and political implications of the views we were committed to.
Should we not, in other words, look away from English teaching and
look at schools, educational organization and society?[6]

[6] James Britton quoted in *The Times Educational Supplement*, 26 November 1971.

This is exactly what I am arguing. Recently a group of scientists have tossed to one side their numbing tradition of neutrality to fight against pollution. It is time now for English teachers to declare their terms. In the last section of this book I will return to the need for a vigorous and articulate politics of Education. When conventional politics have become narrowed down to a matter of money negotiations and, as they are tellingly called, 'package deals', it is time for teachers of the subjective disciplines to assert a politics based on the existential needs of man, those essential needs of life which the Renaissance philosophers discarded, the need for meaning, for relationships, for community, for creation, for meditation: the need to find 'the archetype of a human being' which man carries, potentially and prescriptively, within him. But before outlining the possible content of a politics based on cultural premises, I want to show how the existential needs of man can be given form and depth through the imaginative teaching of English and the sensitive training of teachers—for it is from such practical work in the classroom and the tutorial that any emerging politics of English teaching must, ultimately, draw its strength.

PART II

Practice

THREE

The Creative Word

One ought to be independent but not unimpressionable: that wd.
be to refuse education.

Hopkins

It is not inspiration that exhausts one, but Art.

Yeats

The cultivation of poetry is never more to be desired than at
periods when, from an excess of the selfish and calculating
principle, the accumulation of the materials of external life exceed
the quantity of the power of assimilating them to the internal laws
of human nature.

Shelley

We can safely assume that what is now commonly termed 'creative
writing' did not exist in the schools in the nineteenth century. The
notion of an education through art, urging the expression and
gradual refinement of feeling and sensing, would have alarmed
the Victorians, secure in their belief in 'character-training' and in
the utilitarian purposes of learning. It is true that Ruskin, as early
as 1857, urged that the child 'should be allowed to amuse itself
with cheap colours almost as soon as it has sense enough to wish
for them'.[1] But Ruskin's declaration had to slumber for half a
century before its educational implications were to be appreciated
and slowly realized. The obsession for factual knowledge,
abstract and dislocated, blinded the Victorians to the need for an
education of the whole man.

Now what I want is facts. Teach these boys and girls nothing but
Facts. Facts alone are wanted in life. Plant nothing else and root out
everything else.

Perhaps Gradgrind, who in Dickens' words was 'a kind of

[1] Ruskin in *The Elements of Drawing*.

cannon loaded to the muzzle with facts' is a caricature of the utilitarian teacher, but a caricature so impinging at pertinent points on the actuality that we do not distort the truth very much if we infer that *Hard Times* charts courageously the dominant drift of mass education in the middle of the nineteenth century.[2] Matthew Arnold's constant criticism in his reports of 'teaching by rote' and 'mechanical contrivance' together with his fear that 'children were being bewildered and oppressed by a mass of education hastily heaped together', serve to confirm Dickens' polemical indictment of popular education.

By the end of the century approaches, methodologies and attitudes had changed very little; they remained crude, regimental, repressive. The country school portrayed in Flora Thompson's *Lark Rise to Candleford* must have been typical of hundreds of small schools dotted across the country:

> Reading, writing and arithmetic were the principal subjects, with a scripture lesson every morning, and needlwork every afternoon for the girls . . .
> The writing lesson consisted of a copying of copperplate maxims. 'A fool and his money are soon parted'. 'Waste not, want not'. 'Count ten before you speak', and so on. Once a week composition would be set, usually some recent event. *This was regarded chiefly as a spelling test.* (My italics)

Flora Thompson describes the children settling down to such routine work with an arresting metaphor: 'Once started, they were like a watch wound up, and went on for hours and hours'. Mass education had come to resemble Newton's universe, once set in motion by the Divine Mechanic, continuing passively to repeat the set patterns till the end of time. It had also come, as first Dickens and, later, D. H. Lawrence perceived with almost visionary intensity, to resemble the ugly and inexorable system of

---

[2] It is illuminating to note that Dickens' analysis of Gradgrind is similar to Mill's analysis of Bentham, that influential but highly limited member of the Rational Englightenment. Mill writes: 'He had never been made alive to the unseen influences which were acting on himself, nor consequently on his fellow creatures. Other ages and other nations were a blank to him for purposes of instruction. He measured them by but one standard; their knowledge of facts, and their capability to take correct views of utility, and merge all other objects in it . . . He saw accordingly in man little but what the vulgarest eye can see; recognized no diversities of character but such as he who runs may read. Knowing so little of human feelings, he knew still less of the influences by which those feelings are formed: all the more subtle workings both of the mind upon itself, and of external things upon the mind, escaped him; and no one, probably, who in a highly instructed age, ever attempted to give a rule to all human conduct, set out with a more limited conception either of the agencies by which human conduct *is*, or of those by which it *ought* to be influenced'. (*Essay on Bentham*).

industrial mass production. At the beginning of the twentieth
century it was, therefore, to prove difficult for a tiny minority of
creative teachers to propound the need of an education based on
imaginative and aesthetic principles. Responding to the
innovations urged by Caldwell Cook, Dorothy Owen and others,[3]
a teacher wrote a letter of shocked protest to *The Times
Educational Supplement:*

> It is hardly necessary to mention the possibility of excessive and
> precocious stimulation of the emotions, a danger all the greater now
> that we aim at making our pupils recreate the poem for themselves.
> (April 1920)

Gradgrind had survived his century! The letter also shows how the
seeds of the Rational Enlightenment had drifted over the
centuries to settle in the deep recesses of general consciousness—for it was Locke who had written in *An Essay on
Understanding*: 'figurative speech serves but to insinuate wrong
ideas, move the passions and thereby mislead the judgement'. On
such harsh and narrow premises, poetry could only deteriorate
into an obscure and private matter, at best a matter of 'agreeable
fancies',[4] at worst a matter of psychopathic indulgences.[5] The
teacher's letter, objecting to creative modes of teaching, reveals
how Locke's prejudice had congealed, through the decades, into
hard doctrine.

As early as 1912, Caldwell Cook had sketched some of the
principles on which the alert English teacher and the responsive
primary-school teacher now spontaneously work. 'Quite 70 per
cent of our secondary schoolboys', wrote Cook, 'can write
creditable poetry and all you have to do is to give them
permission.' The insight is *there,* and yet considering the remark
sixty years later, it needs re-formulation. Why the figure 70 per
cent? Why the word 'creditable', implying an adult standard of
evaluation, implying set measure and pattern? Why not the
universal principle: *all children have an innate desire to
symbolize their experience and poetry is one of the most sensitive*

---

[3] For a detailed examination of this movement see David Shayer's *The Teaching of
English in Schools 1900-1970.* I have drawn heavily from this book in the above account.
For another account of the development of imaginative writing in schools see Denys
Thompson's postscript to *Children as Poets* (Heinemann Educational Books).

[4] Descartes saw poets as 'those whose minds are stored with the most agreeable fancies,
and who can give expression to them with the greatest embellishment and harmony'.
(*Discourse on Method*).

[5] For a brief examination of anti-art see Chapter 5.

means of symbolization? And yet, in the context of the educational system which surrounded him, Cook's assertion was revolutionary,[6] as were the teaching-methods he listed in his *Playbooks:*

> 1. Proficiency and learning come not from reading and listening, but from action, from doing and from experience.
> 2. Good work is more often the result of spontaneous effort and free interest than of compulsion and forced application.
> 3. The natural means of study in youth is play.

Such teaching methods, so startling when first advocated, have become today the almost facile commonplaces of educational theory. Indeed, as I indicate throughout this book, I believe we have reached a point where we must not deny the place of play and freedom in education, but yet need to complement it with the notion of structure and direction. As I have argued in the opening chapter, the act of individual innovation presupposes an inherited culture (transmitted partly through reading and listening, which form valuable experiences: Caldwell Cook's division between action and literacy is spurious). And education, likewise, presupposes a context where a fund of materials is freely available and where a climate of trust, concern and disinterestedness prevail. Schools should provide those cultured contexts in which concentrated play (not casual play) becomes possible for all.

At the time, however, at the beginning of the century, the various emphases of Caldwell Cook were polemically sound. Freedom needed to be asserted against compulsion; spontaneity against the inertia of settled habits; the powers of the active imagination against those of the passive memory.

In 1920 Dorothy Owen provided a subjective principle to the movement towards imaginative writing, a principle which, I suspect, she largely derived from the writings of Wordsworth. She urged that the teacher should 'think to make the child think of the image and let the words come'. For the most part, in her book *The Child Vision,* Dorothy Owen regards the image as the sensational recall of experience, of 'the wonder of fresh sights and

---

[6] In drawing particular attention to Caldwell Cook I am following in the footsteps of David Shayer (see *The Teaching of English in Schools 1900-1970*). I may be over-emphasizing his influence. Marjorie Hourd, for example, has written to the author: 'I always like to take the child writing movement back to Quiller-Couch — *The Art of Writing* (1916) — because his just move was to allow for verses in the language 'sucked in with our mother's milk' — instead of in Latin — and he saw so clearly that originality comes from the study of excellence in others'.

scents and sounds', of, for example, 'the feeling of the air when the trees begin to get dark'. The English teacher's task was to discard the set classical models and to encourage the child to express his unclouded vision and so preserve it from prejudice, abstraction and received opinion. At some points in her argument, however, a much deeper understanding of the image is revealed, an understanding strangely in accord with the theories of psycho-analysis which were still being formulated at the time she was writing. She writes:

> There are deeper levels where impressions registered many years ago exercise silent influences without necessarily ever coming to the surface at all . . .
> Words must first be made the servants of images and the mastery will not be complete until subconscious thought becomes articulate. The word will then *hold in itself* the experience and be pregnant with the meaning which it, instead of the images, now encases.

Such formulations implying the transformation of energy into image, image into word, word into meaning, remain fifty years later, central to our understanding of the value of writing in education. It is also fascinating to note that Jung, who was later to influence Herbert Read's seminal book on creativity, *Education Through Art*, was, at the same time, discovering the integrating powers of the image. In his autobiography, reflecting on the years 1912 to 1920, Jung wrote:

> To the extent that I managed to translate the emotions into images—that is to say to find the images which were concealed in the emotions—I was inwardly calmed and reassured . . .
> The images of the unconscious place a great responsibility upon a man. Failure to understand them, or a shirking of ethical responsibility, deprives him of his wholeness and imposes a painful, fragmentariness on his life.

In drawing attention to the importance of the image Dorothy Owen's work clearly anticipates the writings of Herbert Read, Marjorie Hourd, Marion Milner, David Holbrook and many others who have celebrated the image-making capacities of the mind.

When, in the year following the publication of *The Child Vision*, George Sampson suggested that children should be encouraged to write in free verse (a freedom conspicuously lacking in Caldwell Cook's theories) all the main elements for a radically new form of English teaching had been defined, albeit more by chance than design. It was time now for the various elements to be drawn together into a coherent movement. Insights cast by the Romantic poets, by the psycho-analysts (particularly Freud and Jung) and by the creative teachers needed drawing together into a coherent philosophy.

In 1943 Herbert Read's *Education Through Art* was published, in 1948 Marion Richardson's *Art and the Child,* in 1949 Marjorie Hourd's *The Education of the Poetic Spirit.* In the sixties came a further selection of books on English teaching as a creative discipline, as well as anthologies of children's poetry (edited by Boris Ford, Alec Clegg and others), all confirming and amplifying the earlier pioneering works. A gentle revolution seemed at hand. And yet, although the movement pointed continually to *the prospective nature of education* there was soon a danger that the new freedom might become divorced from purposes and so slide imperceptibly into the casual wash of permissiveness which, in the sixties began to be mechanically and ruthlessly pushed forward by the commercial media.

II

'There is no doubt', wrote Herbert Read, twelve years after the publication of *Education Through Art,* 'that a devastating indictment of conventional methods of education can be drawn up. The danger which then ensues is that the bad old method is discarded and no new method is put in its place. Freedom from the past tyranny may be achieved, but no alternative concept of discipline is established. If the children of the past have become neurotic adults because of the systematic repression and frustration practised on them by their parents and teachers, *the children of the future are threatened by an equally bad neurosis because they have not been initiated into any principle of growth or integration'.*[7] (My italics)

In many ways, our young are now acting out that neurosis — a neurosis which the adult world has created by failing to provide moral and imaginative stepping stones and which, for commercial reasons, the mass media is only too happy to sustain and exploit.[8]

[7] Herbert Read in *The Grass Roots of Art* (Faber & Faber).

[8] Consider, for example, the implications of a recent advertisement in the *Sunday Times Colour Supplement.* An old couple are shown with the wife commenting, 'My Ernie thinks that pop concerts are plain evil. And as for those sex films they should be put down'. A young couple reply, 'Ernie should stop thinking'. The advertisement can best be

Have we moved too abruptly from repressive modes of teaching, leaving our children in a moral and cultural vacuum, allowing them only a negative form of freedom? There is, I feel, some truth in it. Our task as English teachers is to take the new freedom and to give it form, meaning and direction. We must endeavour to fashion *disciplines* which are imaginative, *structures* which are open, *forms* which are living. If there has been a tendency in the past to over-value the teacher, there is a tendency now to undervalue him. And this, while it is a healthy reaction against Gradgrind and the innumerable dull and inept teachers throughout the ages, is, yet, destructive—for in our demoralized culture, where values and beliefs have been systematically inverted, the *potentia* of the children can often only be released and developed through the teacher's knowledge, understanding and care. Exclude the teacher, exclude the imaginative discipline, and the result quickly becomes, in drama, the ceaseless regurgitation of last night's television and, in writing, the instant stapling together of pulp-fiction horrors and the idiocies of Radio 1. I have been told of classes that, left to their own resources in drama ('Make up any play you like') always inserted a commercial between acts on the assumption that a break for advertising formed an intrinsic part of the drama.[9] In such an addled environment, the actual qualities and powers of the teacher become all important.

The teacher must be conscious of the nature of a subjective discipline. He must possess a marked feeling for the imaginative process, that process through which we gently symbolize our world and so come to possess it. He must, because the medium of poetry and of teaching is words, have a love of living language, of rhythm, of imagery (and the inward world it portrays) and a ready ability to discriminate between the genuine and the synthetic, the honest and the slick, the original and the stereotyped. It is the teacher's feeling for words, sensed by the class in the way a poem is read out, the way a particular line in a poem is pin-pointed, that quickly spreads to the class—for children do, in spite of all I have said about the extent of cultural

understood, perhaps, by comparing it to the film, proclaimed by Charles Reich in *The Greening of America*, *Wild in the Streets* 'which invited teenagers to put LSD in the water supply, take over the country and cart all people over 30 to thought-remoulding camps'.

[9] Given that 'advertising is locked firmly into the communications system' (Denys Thompson introducing Fred Inglis' *The Imagery of Power*) the assumption is quite reasonable but, of course, such an assumption entails the death of culture i.e. *true* communications.

debasement, naturally delight in the textures and expressive possibilities of their mother-language. Given the right context in the classroom, they are only too willing to experiment, to innovate, to create, to present themselves to the world through their own symbolic forms.

As teachers of English we need, perhaps, to cultivate a more sober view of inspiration. Rudolf Arnheim in an essay on inspiration, wanting to erase indulgent and popular misconceptions about art, wrote that:

> His [the Artist's] method of getting away from 'himself' is not that of distraction but profound concentration, which requires severe discipline of all mental powers and gives shape and depth to his pronouncements.[10]

Given such an understanding of inspiration as a state of concentration and not of distraction, what should be the approach of the teacher in encouraging creative work in writing, art, drama, music and dance? In her pioneering book *Art and the Child* (1948) Marian Richardson described her function as teacher in the following way:

> We were, then, interdependent, and although I was as self-effacing as I could be, I knew that the children relied upon me rather as an orchestra relies upon its conductor.
>
> They would say that I opened a door for them. This meant that they preferred to be given a subject rather than find their own. Once in possession of the all-necessary mind-picture to which my description gave birth, they were directed, steadied and settled. Every moment of the lesson was purposefully spent *while if called upon to work without such guidance they would try first one thing and then another and in the end achieve little or nothing at all.* (My italics)

The notion of the teacher as the settling, conducting, co-ordinating, inspiring influence does not negate the truth locked in Caldwell Cook's epigram, 'The natural means of study in youth is play'. All constructive play, where the being of man delights in its own expressive energies, takes place within a specific context, within a defined space and a certain lapse of

---

[10] Rudolf Arnheim, *Towards a Psychology of Art* (Faber & Faber).

time. It is the task of the creative teacher to provide the settled context within which inspiration becomes possible.[11]

How, then, given the need to draw together form and freedom, spontaneity and direction, can we develop children's creativity with regard to the written word? How in the wasteland left by the demolition of the old can we initiate the principle of growth and integration? I wish now to turn to these questions in detail and in a thoroughly practical manner.

III

How, then, are we to initiate the imaginative discipline with a class — say, anywhere between the ages of nine and thirteen — unfamiliar with creative writing?

The reader may remember that in her small book, *Intensive Writing*, Margaret Langdon offered this opening. Very quickly, at the outset of the lesson, she suggested, assert that there is a spider on the desk and then, without further procedure, ask the children to scribble down their responses to the following questions:

What do you feel about it?
What do its legs look like?
What does its body look like?
It's moving! — How does it move?
What are you going to do with it?

By a series of swift open-ended questions the teacher is urging the child to imaginatively apprehend the spider, to spontaneously describe it and dramatize his feelings towards it. The following are characteristic pieces coming from such work:

> It's body is like a wollen ball
> It's thin fragile legs like pins
> It scurries over the table and scrambles over the books.
> It's tiny body makes me facinated
> I'll let it scurry away or to make a web.

(NERYS JONES, *First Form, unrevised first copy*)

[11] John Richardson, a primary-school teacher, defined the discipline required by teachers as follows: 'I simply mean that teachers should be aware of what they intend to do, of what they should avoid, of the nature of the being they have before them, and of the future development of that being in relation to his present experiences . . . To teach 'in the best modern way' is to cause no split between intellect and ardour. It is imposing a negative attitude on the profession to say that this cannot be taught, or that it can be learned. Rather it is a process of realization which every classroom must foster'. A notion of sensitive and explorative discipline which is central to the present book.

Spider

Ugh! I don't exactly feel frightened of it,
But for some reason I don't want to approach it.
It has long hairy legs, that look like spindles,
And a stubby rounded body that's a deep jet black.
He moves so fast that in a second he will be gone.
I pick up my slipper and bang! wham!
A mess on the wall.

(RUTH LANGDON, *Second Form, final copy*)

Its body looks like hard round orange.
Its legs are like pieces of thin string.
It moves one foot and then the other one.
Oh I drown him!
Oh poor thing!

(SHIRLEY EVANS, *First Form, final copy*)

Or, taking a photograph of a bird,[12] one might impulsively
throw out a series of questions such as the following:

What do my eyes see?
What does my brain think?
What are my wings for?
What are my claws for?
What does my beak do?

Here are the quick responses of two eleven-year-old children to
these questions:

I am a hawk.
I look at the world.
like a map
from above.
my small brain
thinks of
the mice
and shrews
all awaiting
to be killed.

[12] I have used the head of the hawk reproduced in *English Broadsheets 1* (*First Series*) in
this way.

My wings soar
each side
of me.
They glide
and drop
to the
uneven ground.
My talons
grab and rip
and tear.
They now lock
a branch
of a tree
My bloody hooked beak
like an umberella's handle
To feed my beautifull
adorable young.

(NERYS JONES, *First Form, unrevised first copy*)

Hawk

I am a hawk,
My eyes look like jelly.
My small brain thinks how will I catch dinner.
My wings are for hovering.
My claws are for killing.
And my beak is for pricking.

(DENZIL EVANS, *First Form, unrevised first copy*)

It is a simple beginning. What may we have achieved? In the first place we have introduced the active, the inward and the imaginative discipline as opposed to the passive and external memory discipline. Our method has implied that a spider or a hawk (or any other insect, bird or animal) can be a perceived through the imagination and that what is seen, felt, sensed, can be conveyed quickly and dramatically in words. We may also have unobtrusively demonstrated that a small scrap of writing which doesn't rhyme and isn't about sunset or melancholy can possess both poetic intensity and a telling precision of detail.

Another situation which can be taken at this early and undeveloped stage of the work is the simple event of catching a fish (or, perhaps, trapping an animal). Once again, the task is to recreate imaginatively a specific incident as briefly suggested by the teacher:

You are there by the edge of the water.
You are holding the line.
You feel it move, jerk.
There is a fish on the hook!
You haul it in.
You hold it in your hands.
What does it look like?
How does it move?
What are your feelings?

The Battle developed from out of the hurried jottings to such questions. It is fascinating to observe how in this piece the boy, faithfully following his own imaginative impulses, moves out of his own identity in an attempt to enter the sensations of the fish.

The Battle

Silent! Still! The innocent fish moving smoothly through the water. His water. Then through his tiny black glassy eyes the fish sees a worm. Food! This thought and this thought alone flashed through the mind of the creature. Then with sharpness equal to steel he shot forward, his wide gaping mouth closed around the apparent worm. Pain such as he had never felt before made every part of his slippery body scream in utter torment. Writhing, wriggling, he was jerked mercilessly up into—nothing. The man creature then held him tightly in his strong, solid hands. One blast of agony later as the man wrenched the hook from the bleeding mouth of the fish, he was thrown into a rough spiky basket. Dead!

(ADRIAN, *First Form, final copy*)

The experience is convincingly rendered through an imaginatively felt series of sharp sensations which, marvellously, extend even to the texture of the basket ('rough spiky'). How right that the air, our medium, is sensed as 'nothing' and the man seen 'out there' as alien, 'the man creature'. In the writing of such a passage, the child is simultaneously expressing and refining his imaginative perception of the world.

I have suggested, so far, three specific incidents, simple, dramatic, tangible, which form an introduction to the imaginative discipline. Many other situations could be taken and developed along similar patterns. But it is important that the activity generated doesn't stop here—for the work is too tightly structured by the teacher, and the possibilities, while well realized

by most children, are still limited. To move forward, to make
deeper, more personal and more complex, the teacher must offer
a greater range in subject-matter and more freedom for
expression. He needs also to introduce, subtly and slowly, various
forms of writing with which the children can experiment. I wish
now to take each of these developments in turn.

The range of the work can be broadened, quite simply, by
presenting stimuli which by their very nature demand a more
sustained and deeper involvement. The teacher can, for example,
present various myths from the Greek, Hebrew, Celtic and Norse
traditions. He can ask the child to imagine that he is Theseus
tentatively feeling his way down the dark labyrinth towards the
waiting Minotaur. Or that he is Icarus anxious to escape from the
tower, as in the following poem:

Flying

I am on the rim of the grey tall tower,
My white feathered wings each side of me,
The roaring blue sea is like a swaying carpet.
I look at the snow white clouds like balls of cotton wool.
I take my feet off the stone steps and flap the strange wings.
The sea is churning like hot broth in a witch's cauldron.
I look at the sun like a red hot ball.
I ascend slowly.
I go nearer and nearer to the golden face.
Sweat tumbles down my forehead, like a narrow clear waterfall.
The wax is melting. It scalds my arms.
I panic!
The white feathers are dropping like snow flakes.
I fall like a stone.

(NERYS ANNE JONES, *First Form, final copy*)

The teacher may also introduce themes based on historical
experience: the child is a doctor during the years of the Great
Plague, he is a man being executed for treason, he is a scientist
discovering a new planet, he is a chimney-sweep in the nineteenth
century. To stimulate and make the work imaginatively precise,
the teacher will need to draw on a rich mass of materials,
descriptions, facts, interpretations, diaries, letters, poems, songs,
images and symbols. It is not, then, difficult to extend the
range of the work and, in extending the range of the work, the
teacher is, at the same time, granting imagination more freedom:
more freedom for the child to choose where to identify, what or

who to become: more freedom, also, for him to symbolize his inner preoccupations — and this is most important for it is the only way in which children can integrate difficult, painful and elusive feelings into their identities. Consider, for example, how the following poem confronts and makes accessible an experience which, so easily, could be cut off from the conscious personality.

Uncle Dying

My uncle died this last year
A big pity it was
I never thought it would happen but it did.

It was terrible.
My mum nearly fainted
My aunt came down
And my other aunt came from round the corner.

It was frightening, terribly frightening
The undertaker came and took him away.
My dad was there, he came wandering into the kitchen dazed
I wish my uncle was here.

(MARTYN DILLON, *Third Year, final copy*)

The writing of such intimate poems is fundamental to our work[13] for they develop and enhance the true life of the feelings and promote, in however obscure and dark a manner, that process of individuation[14] essential to all healthy forms of life.

It is important that the teacher, having introduced simple structures for imaginative writing based on open-ended questions, is ready to initiate lessons which have virtually no content and as few preconceptions as possible. Such lessons challenge the children to create directly from their own resources. Indeed, such lessons form a prelude to the sort of open classroom (only possible when an implicit understanding of the imaginative process, and the disciplines it entails, has become a possession of most members of the class) which one is moving, slowly and seldom easily, towards. The teacher may take into the classroom, for example, Stravinsky's *The Rite of Spring* and play the first

[13] Some teachers give their children a private book for the writing of any poems, songs, stories, comments that they wish at any point, unprovoked by the teacher, to write. This would seem an excellent idea, for it preserves in the very public world of the classroom both spontaneity and privacy.

[14] This, of course, is Carl Jung's term for the development of the whole personality.

five minutes while the children are asked to jot down whatever the music suggests. The following contrasting passages were written from the images and feelings suggested by the fourth movement of Mahler's *First Symphony*:

Mental Torment

My mind aches and throbs against my skull
Like the rhythmic beating of drums.
Useless thoughts cram through my head
Until sweat beads my brow and trickles down my face.
Despair, — a sorrowful word and true for me.
Forsaken by men and needing some faith in God.
What hope is there now?
Show me a sign, that I may believe?
Lead me to someone who can tell me the truth;
Give me proof . . . I'm afraid to die.

What ecstasy to have an easeful mind,
What peace and perfect serenity.
Fear will be as a cloud torn in a storm,
And death an adventure to encounter.

(JANETTE BROOKS, *Fifth Form, final copy*)

The Tidal Wave

The tidal wave sweeps across the country.
In its wake it leaves a path of destruction.
Citizens flee from their deadly enemy,
While their homes crumble, in the rush of water.

When it calms down, there is nothing left,
Only miles of water, and ugly ruins.
Bodies are floating on the surface of the water,
The lucky ones come back, to find out that everything is gone.

The danger is past, they start clearing up,
They mourn their dead.
Their life is ruined
By a mighty rush of water.

Everyone is weeping,
Everyone is mourning.
The town is silent;
Not a sound is to be heard.

(ROBERT HUGHES, *First Form, final copy*)

God Made This World To Love

Birds of the air and animals of the jungle battling for command. The
eagle swoops down on the lion and kills him for revenge of his sons.
The wise owl and the son of the lion have a talk over peace but the
lion refuses and eats the owl. Then God comes down from heaven as
half-mammal and half-bird and everybody stops fighting and
suddenly realize that they should love one another.

(ANWEN JONES, *First Form, unrevised first copy*)

Paintings and pictures may be used in a similar fashion. In
English Broadsheets I have often reproduced pictures which are,
in important ways, incomplete and, therefore, demand that the
onlooker enter the action in order to complete it. On one
Broadsheet there is a drawing of a boy running. The boy is
obviously terrified. *But what of? Who is he running from? Who is
he running to?* The picture, giving no answers to the questions it
raises, precipitates a personal and imaginative response. Another
Broadsheet reproduces a photograph of a group of boys. They
are huddled together. We cannot see their faces. One is holding a
catapult. *Where are they? What are they talking about? What
are they going to do?* The action needs completion — but it may be
developed in numerous unpredictable ways. Instead of set
answers, we find a diversity of response. Instead of mechanical
and schematic extremes (yes/no, either/or, right/wrong) we have
an experiential activity, an activity which seeks through a field of
energies to find its own personal form, its own unique shape. As
with pictures, so with words. The children can be asked, say, to
write down what they associate with various colours: with blue,
red, silver, green, black. From the lists of associations poems, like
the following, may eventually be fashioned:

Red Versus Blue

Amidst the flowing streams of blue two red, living splashes;
A moving stream of lifeless, grey blue
flowing into another lifeless stream of purpley blue.
A green grass blue, a sky blue, a sea blue
All imitating living things;
Streams upon streams of blue, lifeless blue,
Flowing in all directions, mingling and causing more shades of blue.
Streams upon streams of lifeless blue imitating living things;
Dead things pretending to be alive.
We are blue when we ought to be red
We ought to be like those two splashes,

Vivid, outstanding,
Permanently there,
Nothing moves that true blood red
The rivers of drab dead blue flow around you, passing you by.
Oh red, blood red, I know no one who is as red as you.
Red people are avoided,
We, us blue people lock them away.

(YVONNE HINTON, *Fourth Form, final copy*)

So far, then, the teacher has first released imaginative writing
by taking highly circumscribed situations—the spider on the
desk, the hawk looking down, the fish on a hook—and, by
throwing out a structured sequence of open-ended questions, has
urged the child to focus his creative energies. He has then
progressed by, sometimes, presenting incidents from myth and
history and by, at other times, inviting the child's own
experiences. Also he has occasionally worked with shapes,
objects, pictures, music and sounds, urging the child to follow the
paths suggested by his immediate and unmeditated responses. We
can now move forward by delicately introducing, over a period of
months, a variety of poetic forms. If, previously, the class has
been accustomed to traditional English teaching, many of the
children may still feel that there are, basically, two modes of
writing: the rhyming poem and the two-page composition
('regarded chiefly as a spelling test'). It is essential that they now
experience alternative patterns for creative composition: we need
to discover those forms and techniques which will free the child's
own perceptions and preoccupations. This is, of course, the way
in which most practising poets have regarded inherited poetic
forms. T. S. Eliot declared:

> In my earlier years, or rather in the second phase of my development,
> I went through a period of concentrating my attention on experiment
> in metric and language. It may be that to focus my conscious mind in
> this way helped me to release my imagination. For some poets,
> perhaps, this experiment with forms of verse and with varieties of
> expression may remain a permanent preoccupation.[15]

What poetic forms can children assimilate? In what order
should they be introduced? And in what manner?
If the reader will look back at the pieces of writing on the
spider and hawk, he will observe that the running sequence of
questions (What does its back look like?/What does its legs look

[15] Introduction to Edwin Muir's *Selected Poems* (Faber & Faber).

like?/It's moving!—How does it move?) has persuaded many of
the children to place each separate response on a new line. Very
crudely, this is the principle of free verse. In free verse, the line,
as opposed to the metre, forms the unit: each line tends to embody
a distinct movement, it may be an action, a thought, a
perception, a feeling. With the technique of free-verse at the
forefront of his mind, the teacher could take in the following two
poems translated from Yoruba poetry:[16]

Kob Antelope

A creature to pet and spoil
like a child.
Smooth skinned
stepping cautiously
in the lemon grass.
Round and plump
like a newly married wife.
The neck
heavy with brass rings.
The eyes
gentle like a bird's.
The head
beautiful like carved wood.
When you suddenly escape
you spread fine dust
like a butterfly
shaking its wings.
Your neck seems long,
so very long
to the greedy hunter.

Elephant

Elephant, a spirit in the bush,
Elephant who brings death.
He swallows a whole palmfruit
thorns and all.
He tramples down the grass
with his mortar legs.
Whenever he walks
the grass is forbidden to stand up again.
He tears a man like an old rag

[16] *Yoruba Poetry*, edited by Ulli Beier (Cambridge University Press).

and hangs him up in the tree.
With his single hand
he pulls two palm trees to the ground.
If he had two hands
he would tear the Heaven to shreds.
An elephant is not a load for an old man —
nor for a young man either.

In discussing the poems the teacher can quietly draw attention to the way in which the poems have been written, drawing attention, if it seems necessary, to the more vigorous and condensed lines ('When you suddenly escape/you spread fine dust/like a butterfly/shaking its wings': 'he tears a man like an old rag/and hangs him up in the tree'). I have found that most children quickly assimilate the form of free verse. The following poem was written by an eleven-year-old after reading part of D. H. Lawrence's *Mother Kangaroo:*

A Foal

Born alive!
Sleek, slender;
Brown,
The beautiful face of the foal,
Long thin,
Shining bright eyes.
Tiny ears of a dusty brown,
Look just like leaves on her tiny head.
Her legs are like thin, but soft wood.

Cold!
Hungry
Thirsty
Then, suddenly,
The foal, to great amazement is off.
Skipping,
Frisky
Rolling round the field.
But then drops, falls;
Like an animal dying,
Quiet,
Still,
The foal cuddles in to her mother

Warm!
Silent.
Asleep.

(GIRL. *First Form, final copy*)

The reader will observe for himself how the lines, particularly at
the end, rhythmically enact the movements of the foal. The poem
contrasts with the following passage, written by a girl of about the
same age, where the lines following the slow rhythms of an
inwardly contemplative experience, are long, measured, and
ponderous.

A Candle in the Night

Out in the garden it is black and the wind is howling,
                              then it drops and all goes silent.
Coming down the path, shading my only source of light from the
wind
                    which would quickly extinguish it,
My eyes explore the world around me.
My candle is the only light in what seems eternal darkness,
The heat from my candle warms my frozen fingers.
There is something magical about the eerie shadows it casts
                              upon the silent garden.

The wind drops and I see something moving in the wood beyond the
                              garden.
It has hollow eyes which dance and flicker like my candle-flame.
I watch, unable to move as the little shape slips nearer.
Even when the hot grease burns my hand I cannot move.

I am fascinated by this creature moving towards me.
I turn my head and it rubs around my legs.
I bend to stroke it and a gust of wind extinguishes my candle.
The cat and I are alone in a world of darkness.
And then, as if the curtains of heaven were drawn back, it
                              became lighter.

(CLAIRE. *First Form, final copy*)

A Candle in the Night was written after miming the action of
lighting a candle and carrying it out into a windy night. The
awareness of sensations encouraged by the mime informs the
poem. How vividly the similarity between the cat's eyes and the
candle-flame is drawn — 'it has hollow eyes which dance and
flicker like my candle-flame'. But the theme of the poem, the
strange quest for relationship which, when found, is blessed, at
the end, by the moon breaking through the clouds, reminds us,

once again, that we are not primarily concerned with technique, but with the liberation of the personality through the imagination. The techniques are only valuable when they serve, as they do in this poem, the image-making powers of the mind. The author of this poem at the time of writing seemed incapable of sharing experience with others: she either had to dominate or be painfully alone. In the poem she symbolizes these obsessions. It is significant that in the poem the relationship is with an animal, and yet the darkness is shared: 'the cat and I are alone in a world of darkness'. The image in the last line, which has a visionary quality, is, one feels, pointing the child towards a future in which richer relationships may be formed. *Structures we introduce, which may seem simple and even impersonal to us, are quickly absorbed by the child and triumphantly transformed by his own psychic needs.*

The teacher can move easily and imperceptibly from free verse to Imagism—for in image-writing the image is the centre of energy and tends to form the line. Here, again, the teacher might read out another poem from *Yoruba Poetry:*

Leopard

> Gentle hunter
> his tail plays on the ground
> while he crushes the skull.
>
> Beautiful death
> who puts on a spotted robe
> when he goes to his victim.
>
> Playful killer
> whose loving embrace
> splits the antelope's heart.

During the subsequent discussion of the poem, the teacher could draw attention to the second stanza where the leopard's quiet ferocity is caught, so chillingly, in the image of primitive ritual and sacrifice.

A class of older children might, also, gain by reading Ungaretti's poem *Agony:*

---

[17] Giuseppe Ungaretti, *Selected Poems* (Penguin).
[18] Arthur Waley, *Chinese Poems* (Allen & Unwin).

> To die like thirsty larks
> upon the mirage
>
> Or as the quail
> the sea once past
> having no more
> will to fly
> dies in the first thickets
>
> But not to live on lamentation
> like a blinded goldfinch.[17]

Or the beautifully suggestive poem *Li Fu-Jen:*

> The sound of her silk skirt has stopped.
> On the marble pavement dust grows.
> Her empty room is cold and still.
> Fallen leaves are piled against the doors.
> Longing for that lovely lady
> How can I bring my aching heart to rest?[18]

In these poems and, most particularly, in the Chinese poem, older children can be encouraged to see how in the words of a traditional Chinese poet 'Poetry presents the thing in order to convey the feeling . . . as soon as the mind connects with the thing, the feeling shows in the words'. Here one is moving towards that central principle of imaginative creation, that power of suggestion/feeling/evocation frequently depends on a control of emotion and an accompanying economy of language. Such a principle is best grasped not in the abstract but by a collaborative study of pertinent poems, such as *Li Fu-Jen* and *Leopard.* How is it, the class could be asked, that such brief poems, giving so few details, can yet be so moving, so menacing in the case of *Leopard,* so saddening in the case of *Li Fu-Jen?*

Here are four image poems written by children at different stages of development:

Forest Fire as seen from a Plane

> The flames leap high
> like a red antelope
> continuously jumping.
> Firemen stream like disturbed ants
> Gripping hoses spurting long white streams
> Putting out the blazing trees.

The fire is out,
But the trees stand —
Like black memorial statues,
Dead black ghosts.

(BOY, *Second Form, final copy*)

Candlelight

Soft, warm: a fluttering
Oasis in the desert
Of darkness;
Flickering lights like the
White of flashing eyes;

Luminous, translucent catseyes
In the void of netherness.
Flaming points of spears
In a zodiac army;
Diana's tiny jewels,
Fairer than diamonds.

One flung gold tendril
From a whirling kaleidoscope:
A slender saint with shining
Halo
A white flower in a deep jungle.

(GIRL, *Fifth Form, final copy*)

Spider

From a high ceiling halfway hung,
A master engineer,
On a silver thread.

Not a master of matter.
But an engineer of space.
Outlining in air
Its symmetric web
That traps and kills.

(STUART ADAMS, *Fourth Form, final copy)*

Wood

Wood as a tree.
Wood as a tree in a wood, lowering
Its branches to the earthworm a centipede.
Wood as matches, bursting into a

Scorch of flame — disintegrating into
Bobuls of ash.
Wood as a cross that was massacred.
Wood that was once a sword
That splintered the heart of a
Warrior of Arapahoe, his shoe a
Sacred offering to his mother
Who wept bitterly as it came to life.
And a hut, where stars feel free
To look in and see.

(JANINA NIEDZIELSKA, *Fourth Form, final copy*)

At the appropriate moment, image-writing can turn into work
with riddles for riddles often form densely compressed images as
the following examples from African folk lore show:

We tie a horse inside the house,
    but its mane flies above the roof
                                [fire].

Two tiny birds jump over two hundred trees
                                [eyes].

A beautiful maid in a thorny bush
                    [tongue and teeth].

People run away from her when she is pregnant,
    but they rejoice when she has delivered

                                [gun].

A golden parrot drinking water with its tail
                                [rain].

Riddles, like these, simple and delightful, help the mind to
escape from that symmetrical net of abstractions which education
and technical civilization has persuaded us to throw across our
experience. Riddles proclaim the palpable and sensuous universe
and (implicitly) the primitive connecting energies of the psyche,
revealing 'the observation of affinities/In objects where no
brotherhood exists/To passive minds'.[19]

[19] Wordsworth in *The Prelude*.

Like primitive man, children delight in riddles. The discipline
of the riddle releases their own quick perceptions of the
phenomenal world.

I have an open mouth
and let the sea breeze in.
          [A sea cave]

(JANICE, *Primary School, final copy*)

I have hands that are still
Until a life is put inside me.
          [Gloves]

(JENNIFER, *Primary School, final copy*)

I come out of a hole
in a mist then I stay on the
kitchen wall.
          [Steam]

(JENNIFER, *Primary School, final copy*)

Wet and round. I make no sound
I move on the spot. I have a black dot.
I am always awake except in the night.
I go very bright when I'm in light.
My partner lives over the hill.
          [Eye]

(JANE, *Primary School, final copy*)

Swift as an Arrow

Glittering
Glides swiftly

Among the plants

I was abandoned
Found my way about

Insects scatter as they see me coming
If taken out I would die

I'm silver, gold
Colours of the rainbow
My body plays the scales
As it darts
Hither and thither.

(GIRL, *Second Form, final copy*)

From images and riddles, the teacher can move, at a later
point, to shape-poems which, in an obvious sense, are also

connected with images, but in a visual rather than verbal form.
The teacher will find examples of shape-poems in the works of
George Herbert (*Easter Wings, The Altar*) in Lewis Carroll (*The
Mouse's Tail*), in Apollinaire (see the Penguin selection) and in
Dylan Thomas (the diamond poems). The concentrated habit of
mind we have urged forward in the writing sessions should secure
a batch of work that, as well as ingeniously re-creating the shape
of their subject-matter, also have intrinsic worth as poems.

A Mountain

Snow
c a p
freezing
white, sparklingly
cold. Dissolves when
s u m m e r c o m e s

Flanks. Cold, purple, frosty
mist. Decries a man's significance.

Base. Tepid grey. Tropical warmth.
M a k e s a m a n f e e l v e r y s m a l l.

(GIRL, *First Form, final copy*)

Having broken the line in the shape-poems at many different
stages of sense and sentence construction, the teacher may now
move forward, with a responsive class, to consider the way in
which the line can be used as a sensitive instrument transmitting
the particular pause-and-flow of a poem. A selection of
typographical poems could be discussed with the class, examples
being selected from the work of Cummings and William Carlos
Williams. The children could then be asked to explore the
possibilities of such a technique, using the line and the spaces
between words and lines to convey the pause-and-flow of their
own voices. Here are two very different poems, two distinct voices,
experimenting with typographical techniques. The first is an
attempt to catch the rhythm and emphasis of colloquial speech.
The second, an attempt to catch the rhythms of obsessive and
involuted doubt.

Childhood

Me,
Tich, Mike an' Phil
Had a game of footer

An' knocked it through ole man Tucker's window
So we went into get it out.
'No!' he yelled. 'Get lost!'
                              So we mooched around the back
of 'is garage an' lobbed stones at 'im.
                              Then
'E came out chasin' us so
   We ran round the garages to our den
                  We lobbed stones at 'im
and 'e yelled unrepeatable words
Ya, ya, ya yelled Phil back at 'im.

   Then, someone's 'ead stuck out of
ole man Tucker's window
                 so
we started wavin' at 'im an' 'e
started wavin' 'is fist at us
                 so
             we
      went to 'is garden
                  me
                     an' Phil
      an'
         knocked a few
spuds while
            Tich an' Mike made
      a fire
         The spuds were
great
            but   but
Ole man Tucker told our Mum
         an' she
      'ALF MURDERED ME!

                    (B O Y, *First Form, final copy*)

The Cross

         the cross —
      hope glory Agony Death
      God truth now? when?
      Never gone coming soon
      hope love peace hate
      yes no where? when?
      forced argued accepted dismissed
         Oh God

for the love of God for Christ's sake
in the name of God the Father
And God the son believe in
    heaven
    hell
  eternal life
and die happily to lie under soil
    and stones
         because that's
the end

(HEATHER, *Fifth Form, final copy*)

By fostering an experimental attitude to the freer forms of poetry, we have developed in the children a new awareness of language—lanugage, we have implied by our methods and responses is within us and between us to penetrate, celebrate and share experience. It may now be an appropriate moment for the teacher to present to the children some of the more traditional forms of poetry: the use of repetition, rhyme, parallelism and metre.

To indicate how repetition can enhance the dominant mood of a poem and give it dynamic pattern, the teacher could read out and discuss with the class the following two poems:

The Big Chariot

Don't help-on the big chariot;
You will only make yourself dusty.
Don't think about the sorrows of the world;
You will only make yourself wretched.

Don't help-on the big chariot;
You won't be able to see for dust.
Don't think about the sorrows of the world;
Or you will never escape from your despair.

Don't help-on the big chariot;
You'll be stifled with dust.
Don't think about the sorrows of the world;
You will only load yourself with care.[20]

Praise-Song of the Wind

Trees with weak roots
I will strike, I the wind.
I will roar, I will whistle.

[20] Arthur Waley, *Chinese Poems* (Allen & Unwin).

Haycocks built today
I will scatter, I the wind.
I will roar, I will whistle.

Badly made haycocks
I will carry off, I the wind.
I will roar, I will whistle.

Uncovered shacks of sheaves
I will soak through, I the wind.
I will roar, I will whistle.

Houses not tightly roofed
I will destroy, I the wind.
I will roar, I will whistle.

Hay piled in sheds
I will tear apart, I the wind.
I will roar, I will whistle.

Fire kindled in the road
I will set flickering, I the wind.
I will roar, I will whistle.

Houses with bad smoke-holes
I will shake, I the wind.
I will roar, I will whistle.

The farmer who does not think
I will make to think, I the wind.
I will roar, I will whistle.

The worthless slug-a-bed
I will wake, I the wind.
I will roar, I will whistle.[21]

The Big Chariot while using repetition (the first line remains the opening line of each succeeding stanza) also employs the technique of parallelism, where meaning remains constant but actual phrasing is varied. To *The Big Chariot*, the teacher could add excerpts from the *Old Testament*, and from the works of Walt Whitman and D. H. Lawrence. The following poem, written by an eleven-year-old boy after responding to part of D. H. Lawrence's story *The Man Who Died*, shows a powerful and fascinating use of parallelism:

A-New

As if a Rip Van Winkle
As if a new born child.

[21] An Asian Song translated by Willard Trask in *The Unwritten Song* (Jonathan Cape).

Three days in a wilderness
Three days in perpetual darkness.
More like an interrogation as the sun blazes down,
Let me go to my paradise.
My feet give immense pain
Pain as if an immortal wound.
My eyes do not accept the light,
Everything is a-haze,
As if looking through murky water.
I feel sick with hunger
No food, not a morsal.
My throat is dry.
I feel giddy.
I fall to the ground.

(BOY, *First Form, final copy*)

Finally, the teacher can turn to rhyme and metre: to the creation of ballads and songs. One of the problems with rhyme and metre, is that many children are able to write verses with extraordinary facility, verses which may be technically impeccable, but which are destitute of sense and purpose. Often, children will distort the meaning of their poems in order to secure a regular rhyming system, however obscure, however banal. In the initial work, where children are responding to the quick open-ended sequence of questions thrown out by the teacher, some children will still insist on responding through the artifice of rhyme rather than through emotion. Here, for example, is a response to the questions about the hawk I listed earlier:

I am a hawk
My eyes are looking at mice
They flash like numbers on a dice
I have seen a mouse
I see it like a house.

Even in a very impulsive piece of work the child is rhyming because, in the deep recesses of his mind, *he identifies rhyming with poetry*. He is thinking in rhymes because he believes this to be the essence of poetry. One of the negative functions of presenting a variety of free forms for writing is to weaken the tyranny of this identification, for, until it is displaced, genuine poetry, poetry which transports the unique and heightened perceptions of its author, cannot flourish. Once the identification of creative writing with rhyming has been broken, some children, writing under the sway of strong feelings, will find themselves using rhyme (and repetition) quite naturally, as in the following poem:

Dead Dog

Lying in the nettles
As still as lead
My dog lay dead.
Her mouth was angry
And covered in blood.
I felt very sick.
My brother cried,
'Our dog is dead'
A pool of blood surrounded her head.
She was white as snow.

(BOY, *Third Form, final copy*)

In this poem, the writer is not searching out rhyming words, but is seeking to symbolize and so objectify a disturbed experience. The rhyming (lead/dead, dead/head) is an intrinsic part of the poem, a part of the tissue of feelings and sensations. And this is precisely the understanding we hope to have come to with our class during the first few months of imaginative writing. The teacher may now move, with confidence, into work on ballads, chants and songs.[22]

Slowly, gently, over the months and years, we hope to be moving towards that state where the individual is able to fashion his own style of writing, where the discipline of imagination has become internalized, where the powers of overt guidance diminish and the powers of co-operation and self-critical independence expand.[23]

There remains the danger that we *over*-stress the place of form, structure, discipline and technique, for they, in the midst of impending confusion, are certain and tangible things. We must, therefore, be ready to give as great a weight to the largely intangible and uncertain elements from which the poems we seek to release so often emerge. I want now, briefly, to reflect on the *act*

[22] For examples of poetry by children using repetition, rhyme and metre see my *Teachers' Book* to *English Broadsheets* (First Series) pp. 25, 28, 29, 30, 33 and 34.

[23] This must remain an ideal. The whole chapter should be understood as presenting an ideal schemata for creative work. The aim of other sections of the book is to show how threatened, indeed, how impossible, such an ideal can be in the surrounding context of the consumer-society, which has room neither for ideals nor creativity. It is this very conflict which may create a politics of English teaching, perhaps along the lines suggested in the last section of this book.

of writing. *What happens with the responsive class between the teacher's suggestions and hints for a poem and the moment he collects them in?* What is the nature of the creative process?

IV

We must, as teachers and tutors, be ready to acknowledge that creative work can often, by its very nature, be problematic. Writing a poem or a story can engender frustrations, insecurities, anxieties — and this is so because in any creative activity we are generally moving beyond what we cognitively know to what we don't know (but vaguely sense) and must create. In creative work the child is leaping from the mundane ground towards possibilities that have never been uttered in that particular way, with that particular image and that particular rhythm before. After twenty minutes of effort in which many words had been scrawled down the page, an eleven-year-old boy, in a storm of energy, suddenly deleted everything except:

> Crow —
>   devil's pandar,
> thief of nature —

His aggressive act of revision was inspired by an intuitive appreciation of poetic form and language.

Creating (which may often involve destroying)[24] may sometimes be elating but it can also be difficult and painful. We know this, if not from our own experience and the experience of individual children in the classroom, from the comments made by unusually gifted artists. Here, for example, is how Van Gogh wrote to his brother Theo about his work:

> So you see that I am in a rage of work, though for the moment it does not produce very brilliant results. But I hope these thorns will bear their white blossoms in due time, and that this apparently sterile struggle is no other than the labour of childbirth. First the pain, then the joy.

---

[24] Here I agree with Rollo May, the existential psychotherapist. In *Power and Innocence* he quotes Mondrian: 'My style of painting is this: first I had to annihilate the form by reducing it to lines, colour and circles . . . Then I had to destroy the colour . . . Then I had to tear out the circles leaving only the planes and lines . . . My art consists of the purest possible line and proportion.' But, while being often aggressive, art is essentially an act of reparation, a desire to repair what is broken. The aggressive energies must be subordinate to the creative passion, which unifies and restores.

Though every day difficulties crop up and new ones will present themselves, I cannot tell you how happy I am to have taken up drawing again. I had been thinking of it for a long time, but I always considered the thing impossible and beyond my reach. But now, though I feel my weakness and my painful dependence in many things, I have recovered my mental balance, and day by day my energy increases.[25]

Flaubert wrote in a letter: 'You speak of your discouragements: if you could see mine! Sometimes I don't understand why my arms don't drop from my body with fatigue, why my brains don't melt away. I am leading a stern existence, stripped of all external pleasure, and am sustained only by a kind of permanent rage . . .'[26]

Of course, no teacher will expect this 'order of intense and sustained preoccupation from his class; yet many of the problems described in these letters — of feeling discouraged, of feeling lost, of feeling that the power needed is beyond one's reach — are quite common features of creativity and, particularly so, in adolescence. But if we can encourage, partly through our own responses to the children's difficulties, a frame of mind which relishes the problems, which appreciates the co-existence of a multiplicity of worlds and words that, at high moments, may be drawn together and, at low moments, must remain apart: then we have promoted a response to life which is able to welcome the difficulties in the triumphant spirit of Van Gogh — 'first the pain, then the joy'.

The trouble in Education is that we have failed to ask existential questions. We have asked academic questions (When was this poem written? What sort of style is it written in? Where does it belong in the body of English literature?) but we have not asked such fundamental questions as: What happens when a poem is being shaped? What actually happens in the duration of time between the first conception of the poem and its final completion? How is the person changed by writing it? Literature, we must remember, does not slip from a pre-existential order of essences, but is the assertion of an individual made in time. We need, in brief, to turn our attention to poetry as a living process, as an act of becoming.

[25] Letter from Cuesmes dated 24 September 1880. See *The Complete Letters of Vincent Van Gogh* in two volumes (Thames and Hudson).

[26] Quoted in Rudolf Arnheim's *Towards A Psychology of Art* (Faber & Faber).

Consider, for example, the following worksheet of an eleven-year-old girl writing about an owl.

The Owl

I look around with my enormous eyes
                              shuffle
I listen carefully for every ~~scuffle~~,
And then, a rustling sound in the grass
I look
~~(A mouse)~~ down and see a mouse
My Supper.

        spread   soft
I softly (open) my silk / wings
And noislesly, I fly above
Suddenly I dive and then a squeak.
I have caught my prey.

                              screeching bundle
                              ~~mouse~~
Climbing with my screeching ~~prey~~
I perch on a high branch
Out of all danger.
My prey is teared to pieces
By my strong curved beak and sharp talons.

                    catching
I'm a clever one for ~~caching~~ mice
It's very rare I miss
And also I am agile
With quick movements ~~(and)~~ good hearing and
                              penetrating
                              eyesight.

~~(Some people say I)~~

It is revealing to notice how at the beginning of the second stanza the child first wrote: 'I softly open my silk wings.' Then as she quickly considered it, she must have deleted the verb 'open' and inserted the rhythmically more suggestive and perceptually more accurate 'spread'. The line then read: 'I softly spread my silk wings.' Then she considered (I suggest) the line, now revised, and responding to the new rhythm even so small a change had created (particularly in the run of soft sounds) she suddenly saw what the full line as a poetic movement had to be. Between 'silk'

and 'wings' she inserted the word 'soft' and achieved the final line:
'I softly spread my silk soft wings.'

It is a line that through its rhythm and alliteration beautifully
enacts the owls hushed movements. Here we can see how the girl is
working in the manner of Keats who wrote in one of his letters:
'My judgement is as active while I am actually writing as my
imagination. In fact all my faculties are strongly excited and in
their full play.'

The opening sentence of the next stanza first began:

> Climbing with my prey
> I perch on a high branch
> Out of all danger.

Then she had obviously scrutinized that word 'prey'. It is, of
course, an adequate word (it is used in the previous stanza) but, I
suspect, she wanted to draw closer to the imagined event, to pass,
as is the manner of fine poetry, from the unfelt generality to the
unique particularity. So in her second attempt she scrawls
'mouse': 'Climbing with my mouse.' The detail directs our
attention to the actual — it excludes all those vague possibilities
conjured by the word 'prey' — and yet it is still poetically lacking,
for the imagination wants to meditate *on the trembling state* of
the captured creature, caught, as it is, in the owl's talons. Finally,
the writer, having accepted, then rejected, both 'prey' and
'mouse', inserts 'screeching bundle': 'Climbing with my
screeching bundle'. 'Screeching' evokes the mouse's terror, while
the word 'bundle' expresses, most starkly, its blank helplessness.
The line fuses a high degree of particularity with that peculiar
and inexplicable sense of universality which is the hallmark of all
significant poetry.

T. E. Hulme's definitions of art clarify, at a general level, the
observations I have been making about *The Owl*:

> The motive power behind any art is a certain freshness of experience
> which breeds dissatisfaction with the conventional ways of expression
> because they leave out the individual quality of this freshness. You
> are driven to new means of expression because you persist in an
> endeavour to get it out exactly as you felt it. You could describe art,
> then, as a passionate desire for accuracy, and the essentially aes-
> thetic emotion as the excitement which is generated by direct
> communication. Ordinary language communicates nothing of the
> individuality and freshness of things. As far as that quality goes we

live separated from each other. The excitement of art comes from this rare and unique communication.[27]

The most vivid parts of the *The Owl* illustrate a process in which the perception of an imagined experience is being refined in the single act of writing. The refining is, however, by no means complete. At the end, the reader will have noticed how the poem deteriorates to the level of general prose, merely listing, in the manner of the encyclopedia, other relevant facts:

> And also I am agile
> With quick movements and good
>   hearing and penetrating eyesight.

Yet the final deletion of the closing line: 'Some people say I' points, even here, to a dim realization that the poem is complete, points not only to the beginnings of self-criticism but to an emerging recognition of aesthetic form.

The following poem came in the same batch of work as Lowri's *Owl* and it demonstrates, again, a similar endeavour to condense experience and to give it significant form:

> ~~It slither over rocks~~
> ~~like a~~
>
> It slithers over rocks
> and winds round the boughs
> in the steaming jungle.
> ~~It i~~ Silent like phantom
>   grey like a ghost
>   My penitrating eyes
>   to hipnotize
>   any unwary animals
>   And my darting tounge
>   like the devils fork
> ~~My scales are pr~~
> I swallow eggs
> I crush shrews
> I am ~~the king~~ Satan
> My name is the snake

The deletion of 'It slithers over rocks like a' and then the beginning again points in the same way to a dissatisfaction with impersonal description of the snake, and yet an uncertainty as

[27] T. E. Hulme, *Speculations* (Routledge & Kegan Paul).

how else to 'capture' the animal.[28] Suddenly she sees how it is to
be done through a primary identification with the snake.

> I slither over rocks
> and winds round the boughs.

The poem moves forward with that individual quality of freshness
described by T. E. Hulme to the lines:

> And my darting tongue
> like the devil's fork

and the deletion of:

> My scales are pr

Here it would seem an important juncture has been reached. Her
immediate purpose, following the pattern set by the poem, is to
continue to describe the snake's appearance (movement, eyes,
tongue, scales, etc) but the image 'devil's fork' suggests action,
destructive action and self-assertion. Responding to the
possibilities locked within the image she deletes the half-line on
the snake's scales, and boldly takes the poem in the direction
suggested by her imagery. The sentences become short and
assertive:

> I swallow eggs
> I crush shrews
> I am ~~the King~~ Satan
> My name is the snake.

Again, the deletion of 'the King' and insertion of Satan, is
absolutely right for it is drawn out of all the imagery that has gone
before it: 'silent like a phantom', 'my penetrating eyes/to
hypnotize/any unwary animals', 'my darting tongue/like the
devil's fork'. The identification of the snake with a King would
have weakened the whole poem, putting its imagery at war with
its meaning. Identification with Satan, however, draws the
imagery together within a unifying conception, and completes the
poem.

I have taken a few changes in two poems to show the way in
which children, in a context allowing for both concentration and
spontaneity, can tussle with words in order to articulate their
imaginative experience. It is important that the teacher

[28] Even in the fourth line part of her mind is still thinking in the pattern of I—It. Or is it
that *in the fourth line* she has seen how she can use a first-person narrative?

recognizes the sort of chaos out of which many artefacts of worth and beauty eventually   emerge. Here, we can gain valuable insights by considering the practise of our poets. Trelawny described a first draft of a poem by Shelley as follows:

> It was a frightful scrawl: words smeared out with his finger, and one upon the other, over and over in tiers, and all run together in most 'admired disorder'; it might have been taken for a sketch of a marsh overgrown with bulrushes, and the blots for wild ducks . . .[29]

Mary Shelley in her comment about Shelley's *Posthumous Poems* (1824) indicates that this must have been the disordered state from which most of his poems rose up:

> Did anyone see the papers from which I drew that volume, the wonder would be how any eyes or patience were capable of extracting it from so confused a mess, interlined and broken into fragments, so that the sense could only be deciphered and joined by guesses, which might seem rather intuitive, than founded on reasoning.

Edgar Allen Poe in an article on the creative process referred to 'the elaborate and vacillating crudities of thought, at the true purposes seized only at the last moment, at the innumerable glimpses of idea that arrived not at the maturity of full view, at the fully matured fancies discarded in despair as unmanageable, at the cautious selections and rejections, at the painful erasures and interpolations'.[30] What we have been analysing in the children's poems is a comparable struggle to fashion sincere and aesthetic form. The process of quick revision operating in the *Owl* poem is not dissimilar to that shown in this draft of a poem by Emily Dickinson:

> A little Snow
> was here and there
> Disseminated in her
> Hair —
> Since she and I
> had met and played
> Decade had hastened
>   hurried
> To Decade — gathered

[29] Quoted in Phyllis Bartlett's *Poems in Process* (Oxford University Press).
[30] *ibid.*

> But time had added,
> not obtained
>   invincible inviolate
> Impregnable the Rose
> For summer too
> °indelible — °inscrutable
> too +obdurate — for
>   competent
> Snows —
>   inviolate
> x illustrious the Rose
> x sumptuous — for Snows —
> Impregnable the Rose
> For summer too inscrutable
> too sumptuous for snows — [31]

The quick listing of *possible* words: 'invincible/inviolate/ *impregnable*', 'indelible, *inscrutable,* obdurate': and the sudden latching onto the right word, is exactly what the child is doing as she deletes 'prey', then 'mouse', and finally leaves 'screeching bundle'.

This brief study of first drafts brings me to my final concern — namely, to a consideration of the importance of the poetic process. In the past, in our schools and colleges, we have given too much narrow intellectual attention to the achieved artefacts of literature and too little to an imaginative consideration of the strange and elusive processes by which they were achieved. In some places, literary criticism operates almost in the manner of a practical science: observing, comparing, classifying. The more able adolescents in our schools have learnt set patterns of response to set texts: set novels, set poems, set plays: patterns which, more often than not, have excluded both the poet's creativity and the reader's. The main aim has been to classify the various techniques of the author and then to succinctly place him in one of the various leagues of academic merit. We have not given enough attention to the act of creation — and the consideration of the value of creativity in the forging of identity, the making of relationships, and the development of cultural life.

---

[31] The last three lines would seem to form the final choices for the second stanza which would thus read, keeping Emily Dickinson's lines:

> 'But time had added,
> not obtained,
> Impregnable the Rose
> For summer too inscrutable
> too sumptuous for snows'.

And, no doubt, one of the reasons for this failure is due to the anxiety and shock that we can often feel when confronted with the uncertain, with, say, the page of scribble where the disorganized sentences run beyond the laws of syntax into unlikely meanings. Charles Lamb reacted to the original copy of Milton's *Lycidas* with precisely the sort of anxiety I have in mind:

> How it staggered me to see the fine things in their ore, interlined, corrected as if their words were mortal, alterable . . . as if inspiration were made up of parts, and these fluctuating, successive, indifferent! I will never go into the workshop of any great artist again.

Lamb clearly wanted to imagine the poem as if it had descended from a divine order.[32] He was perturbed to discover its earthy origins, its impeded stumbling towards order and beauty. Yet, today, when we tend to locate the origins of the divine and the demonic in man's psyche, it is precisely such a courageous tussling with the dim and bright energies to create enduring form, which we should admire and seek to emulate. For these reasons I agree wholeheartedly with Keat's proposition: 'We read fine things but never feel them to the full until we have gone the same steps as the author'. And I assent to the proposition in two ways. First of all, it is illuminating to trace, where it is possible, the origins and development of a particular poem, in order to sense something of that fire in which fine poetry is hammered into shape. Secondly, it is essential that the child and, later, the student of the subjective and aesthetic disciplines, through his own efforts to make artefacts, becomes aware of the difficulties, delights, and, above all, the values of the creative process.

An opening paragraph of a fragment of autobiography, written by a College of Education student, displays a number of the qualities I would like to draw attention to.

> Again and again she probed back, trying to piece the fragments of colour, people, places and warmth into a comprehensible pattern. They merged for a moment, only to be lost again in a shifting mist. Again she reached out and grasped a memory and lost it. What emerged finally, perhaps covered a space of four years, but time itself was irrelevant, as the events could have been separated by minutes, hours or months.[33]

---

[32] Earlier on in the same commentary Lamb had written 'I had thought of the Lycidas as of a full-grown beauty — as springing up with all its parts absolute'.

[33] For the full context see my *Autobiography in Education:* Section 3 (Heinemann Educational Books).

The writer is anxious to discover a comprehensible pattern in her early experiences, to find a recognizable landscape beneath a shifting mist. But the short passage can also be understood at a more general level as a metaphor for the artist's quest, for the quest, that is, to discover (partly through the act of creation) an underlying symbolic pattern beneath the seemingly disconnected and arbitrary events of life.[34] Such an effort can be remorseless ('again and again': 'again she reached out and grasped a memory and lost it') and yet it is, at the same time, a delicate task (like trying to piece fragments of colour) and, always, the object sought is liable to elude the seeker.

The teacher will not expect to find in children's work the same degree of self-consciousness as is manifested in mature writing. Poems, especially those written by children below the age of thirteen, are often written impulsively, and spontaneously possess a remarkable symmetry (as, for instance, the poems *The Fox* and *The Panda* quoted in Chapter 1). Even the revisions, like the ones we have commented on in the *Owl* and *Snake* poems, are generally made in an impulsive manner. Yet they reveal the beginnings of self-criticism, the first tentative movements towards a conscious appreciation of harmony. It is important for the teacher and later the tutor (in the universities and colleges) to develop these early impulsive judgements but always in relationship to the particular child and the particular poem. We must not sever the critical habit from the creative source (this, sadly, is what happens, at the moment, under the pressures of 'A' level and academic university studies). Perhaps it should be our long-term aim to make criticism creative and to make creativity, at least at the stages of expression, self-critical — which is only to reaffirm what the Romantics since the time of Coleridge and Schiller have demanded, that we should nurture the whole man through the power of the aesthetic disciplines.

I hope in this chapter to have given some practical and theoretical indications as to what such a development of the whole person might mean in relationship to the discipline of imaginative writing in the classroom. I now want to show how man's primary need to symbolize and ritualize experience, which I have argued forms our working assumption in the classroom, is being constantly manipulated and largely savaged by commercial forces

---

[34] Carl Jung would have described the quest as a search for a myth through which one could live.

in our society. I wish now to examine not the genuine poetry of
the human spirit, but the counterfeit mass-produced poetry of
materialism.

FOUR

Against the Counterfeit Culture

In contemporary America, children must be trained to insatiable
consumption of impulsive choice and infinite variety. These
attributes, once controlled, are converted into cash by advertising
directed at children. It works on the assumption that the claim that
gets into the child's brain first is likely to stay there.

Jules Henry

The formulation of experience which is contained within the
intellectual horizon of an age is determined, not so much by events
and desires, as by the basic concepts at people's disposal for
analysing and describing their adventures to their own
understanding.

Susanne Langer

I am convinced that happenings no longer happen; instead the
clichés operate spontaneously.

Karl Kraus

I

I have argued that the main task of English teaching is to develop
an imaginative discipline, a discipline that will provide a framework within which children can come to possess their own
experience through the creative and integrating power of the
symbol. I have suggested that it is also the intention of the teacher
and part of the discipline he seeks to establish, to relate the varied
expressions and images of the child to a common heritage of
literature, which constitutes a major part of the embodied life-
wisdom of the human race. I have briefly indicated that such a
discipline can be interpreted as an elaboration of the relationship
between the mother and infant where an elementary but essential process of innovation and tradition, spontaneity and
interpretation, takes place all the time. And just as the success of
the mother-infant relationship relies on an encompassing trust,

so, I have implied, is it in the classroom and in the tutorial; children and students will only present themselves through their writing, art and drama if they are inwardly convinced that the teacher or tutor will respect and attend to both what is seriously created and what it may signify. In brief, *English teaching as a subjective discipline presupposes the inter-relation of three primary energies: the need to symbolize, the need for culture and the need for trust.*

It is urgent that we now consider the way in which these primary energies are exploited and perverted in our society — for long before the child enters school and continuing long after he has left it another and more powerful educational force is at work, invading the mind and littering it with cliché, slogans and stereotyped expectations. We must never forget that the intention of the persuasion industry, manufacturing heroes and heroines, is to firmly imprint brand names on the still soft wax of the child's mind before he has even mastered words with which to reflect. As an official for a cereal product has put it, 'We began to sell children our product before they could talk. They know who the TV characters are long before they can say full sentences . . . Now they tell their mothers what to buy. Their mothers don't tell them'.[1]

Television is the instrument which makes possible such a mass indoctrination of the young, the creation of pseudo-myths and empty symbols being the means. Plato's disquiet lest his guardians be 'fed on images of vice like poisonous weeds, culling and cropping large quantities every day in little bits from all sides until they unconsciously collect one great mass of corruption in their souls'[2] has become through the technological revolution in mass-communications, a sinister reality, particularly in America. The true symbolic heritage of nursery rhymes, myths and fairy tales, recreating the journey of life from birth to marriage to death, with its inherent conflicts between good and evil, beauty and ugliness, light and darkness, has now been largely superseded by the synthetic creations of the copywriters and commercial entertainers. It is reported that in Los Angeles, for example, the majority of mothers of two-year-old children sing

[1] An official for an American Cereal Product quoted in Ron Goulart's *The Assault on Childhood* (Gollancz).

[2] Plato in *The Republic*.

TV jingles and that at the age of three, nine out of ten can identify all the main cartoon figures.[3]

In this part of the essay I am anxious to stress the symbolic dimension of advertising. It is not sufficient to isolate particular advertisements from their context and to analyse them in terms of information and persuasion (although, as I will show later this is a very good exercise in developing powers of discrimination). It is not even enough to relate advertising to the insatiable requirements of a capitalist economy (though this, too, is important). What we must do, in the first place, is to look at advertising as a symbolic system which, taken as a whole, dramatizes a limited number of responses to experience and conveys, through the methods of poetry, not logic, a fairly consistent interpretation of man's nature. In its widest contours, advertising has to be interpreted as a complex counterfeit culture, generating art forms which, for commercial reasons, spuriously answer such existential questions as *Who am I?* and *How should I live?* If we glance at the characteristic copy of most advertising we invariably encounter the sublime language of religion and of mystical and Romantic poetry. Consider the following excerpts, taken at random, from a number of advertisements:

> *Fabergé made Love and called it Kiku*
> *A Colibri lighter is love*
> *Happiness is a cigar . . .*
> *Xanadu is everything. And beyond everything*
> *Make Hovis your daily bread*
> *The unique sensation awakens the taste buds and prepares you for what you are about to receive.*

One of the distinguishing marks of poetry and religion is that it invests the common objects of daily experience (bread, water, wine, dust, wood, sun, moon, stars) with a strange multiplicity of meanings and associations. Whereas science struggles to establish the precise sign, the mark which has a simple unambiguous reference, art and religion create the symbol, the artefact which concentrates within itself numerous and numinous feelings and meanings (or rather, hints of meaning). It is obvious from the

---

[3] See article on TV Ads in *The Times Educational Supplement* (July 1973). In the same article Roland Kransen points out that in rural Pennsylvania, pre-schoolers watch television for an average of 30 hours a week. *IBA Notes* (March 1973) claims that in Britain 'the average home in this country watches ITV for more than three hours a day, and BBC for more than two hours'.

copy I have quoted that advertising often operates in the manner
of poetry. In *A Colibri lighter is love* a general concept is nailed
into a specific object in the manner of poetry where, as we saw at
the end of the last chapter, particularity and generality are fused
together. In some of the other quotations ('Fabergé made love
and called it Kiku' and 'Make Hovis your daily bread') we hear
echoes of the sublime poetry of the Authorized Version of the
Bible. As S. I. Hayakawa has said, 'the task of the copywriter is
the *poeticizing of consumer goods*'.[4] The experience of ecstasy, of
creating, sharing, loving, is thus constantly and artificially
connected to mass-produced objects: toothpaste, soap, razor-
blades, cigarettes, chocolates, cars, cosmetics: objects which,
needless to say, cannot support the high associations they have
been given. In this way *the true language of cultural
experience—particularly where it incarnates the feelings of love
and tenderness, of mystery and exultation—becomes unutterably
debased.* Hayakawa claims that:

> The unsponsored poet of today works in a semantic environment in
> which almost all the poetry that ordinary people hear and read is the
> sponsored poetry of consumer goods. Poetic language is used so
> constantly and relentlessly for the purposes of salesmanship that it has
> become almost impossible to say anything with enthusiasm or joy or
> conviction without running into the danger of sounding as if you were
> selling something.[5]

The language of positive experience has been so used, so
parodied, so abused by the official poets of industrial society that
the visionary alternatives to that society have become all but
unthinkable.

It is generally acknowledged that dictators, like Hitler or
Stalin, pervert language on such a vast scale, inverting and
changing the meaning of words until no word possesses any
settled sense, that effective resistance is rendered impossible. I
would suggest that advertising, seen as a totality, has similar
repercussions on our culture, depleting symbolic forms so that a
people's perceptions and interpretations become narrowed down
to the confines of the present 'realities', the actualities which exist,
and from which no-one can escape. Perhaps this, indeed, is the
general function of advertising; it exists, not primarily to sell
specific goods, but, first and foremost, to fashion an elaborate

---

[4] S. I. Hayakawa in *Language in Thought and Action* (George Allen & Unwin).
[5] ibid.

mythology, an endless sequence of rituals, chants, ikons, fables, litanies, gods, in order that the present goals of increased productivity, increased power and increased profits become inescapable and thereby perpetuate themselves for ever.

This is not, in any way, an original interpretation, disturbing as it may seem. Denis Thomas in his defence of the persuasion industry, *The Visible Persuaders,*[6] concluded:

> Association with enjoyable sensations gives advertising its decorative glitter and its glamorous aspiration. It is even arguable that this is *its ultimate justification,* as if the economic purpose of commercial persuasion were becoming almost irrelevant compared with *its unceasing effort to gild and glorify the world around us.*

What Denis Thomas fails to point out is that when persuasion becomes so diffuse, so all-pervasive, it becomes even more powerful for it begins to appear as the essential condition for all forms of social communication. In this way, obtrusively (as on ITV and in the glossy colour supplements) or unobtrusively (as with commercially sponsored sport) the questionable assumptions of display advertising and general publicity easily become the informing notions and ruling principles of a whole people. Indeed the actual techniques of advertising, the techniques of simplification, magnification and titillation, begin to spread beyond their boundaries and enter all communications. Intellectuals become super-stars.[7] Christians coin slogans like 'Christ is the solution/to moral pollution'. Politicians exchange 'package deals'. Newspapers for the masses present themselves with crass jingles such as 'The full of fun Sun'. Poetry becomes 'show-biz'.[8] Art turns into 'Pop', and then 'op'.[9] Literature becomes a vehicle for exhibitionism (consider the title 'Advertisement for Myself'[10]). And the reviewing of books and films often deteriorates to a tasting of sweets and perversions.

Yet Thomas's actual conclusion that advertising seeks to gild and glorify the world around us confirms my argument about the overall symbolic function of advertising, as do the following

---

[6] Denis Thomas, *The Visible Persuaders* (Hutchinson).

[7] The heading to a major article on Frank Kermode in *The Times Educational Supplement* was recently headed 'Intellectual Super-star'.

[8] The slogan of Adrian Henri and Co., on a BBC Television poetry programme.

[9] Herbert Read writes: 'The so-called movements — Action Painting in the United States, Pop Art and op Art — have become pseudo-movements, the creation of journalists. See *The Black Rainbow* (Heinemann Educational Books).

[10] Title of a novel by Norman Mailer.

claims made by powerful copywriters and salesmen:

> Our enormously productive economy . . . demands that we make consumption our way of life, *that we convert the buying and use of goods into rituals,* that we seek our spiritual satisfactions, our ego satisfactions, in consumption . . . We need things consumed, burned up, worn out, replaced and discarded at an ever increasing rate.[11]
>
> (My italics)
>
> For all its shortcomings,there must be something discerning (sic) about an industry which deploys so much energy and wit *to publicise the hopefulness of life, incorrigible · faith in little things, indestructible optimism* . . .[12]
>
> (My italics)
>
> Cars are an extension of one's personality. *They are given pet names.* They represent major investments. *Cars are outward symbols of success.* There are still (in Britain) many first car people, who have only now bought their first proofs of having arrived.[13]

We can conclude that one of the main functions of advertising is the attempt to manufacture, with the help of poets, musicians, artists, film-makers, psychologists, behaviourists, sociologists and many others, a continuous mythology which not only elevates consumer objects into symbols but also unifies, through its innumerable creations, a society based on the need to consume, burn up, wear out, replace and discard at an ever increasing rate.

I suggested earlier that the traditional heritage of nursery rhymes, myths, legends and fairy stories are valuable because they 'lighten the inescapable conflicts of childhood with a promise of some security, identity and integrity'.[14] Many of our inherited tales possess a common archetypal pattern: the hero is born, grows up, leaves his mother and father, confronts a series of temptations and ordeals, and having triumphed over them, marries the waiting princess. Such stories clearly symbolize the path of Everyman, etching in bold lines the gradual and ideal journey from infant dependence to maturity. Through the heroes and heroines, children may dimly come to feel that there is a distinct pattern to life, that there are conflicts but also

---

[11] Victor Lebow in *The Journal of Retailing* quoted in Vance Packard's *The Hidden Persuaders* (Penguin).

[12] Philip Stobo, *Advertising Copywriting as a Career* (The Advertising Creative Circle).

[13] Ernest Dichter in *Harvard Business Review.* It is interesting to notice the way in which through the phrase 'many first car people' a consumer object is transformed into an essential attribute of personality.

[14] Erik Erikson, *Childhood and Society* (Penguin).

reconciliations, and that always at the centre of the design there
lies the true self, the promise of identity. Coleridge claimed that
through the early reading of fairy tales his mind 'had been
habituated to the vast' and that there was 'no other way of giving
the mind a love of the Great and the Whole'.[15] It is not, then,
surprising that the false mythologists of the consumer society,
realizing the educative powers of the archetypal story, have been
anxious to disseminate their own fabricated rhymes and legends.

> Children love their heroes and if a hero says 'eat Wheaties' they
> will — for years and years and years. To be able to capitalize on a fad,
> a company has to be able to move in and out fast.[16]

As we have seen, one of the declared intentions is to implant
brand names on the child's mind before he can think, but there is
another aim, less obvious and perhaps not wholly conscious,
which is to constantly symbolize a narrow range of sensational
responses to the world which are wholly in accord with the manic
goals of endless consumption. Here the values and aspirations of
traditional culture, as embodied in myth and fairy tale, the need
for integrity, courage, independence, loyalty, love, are stood on
their head. The artificially engendered myths for children urge,
more often than not, greed, selfishness, conceit and violence.
An American salesman proclaims:

> If you want to create your own hard-hitting spokesman to children,
> the most effective is the super-hero-miracle worker . . . The
> character would be adventurous. And he should be on the right side
> of the law. A child must be able to mimic his hero, whether he is
> James Bond, Superman or Dick Tracy; to be able to fight and shoot
> to kill without punishment or guilt feelings.[17]

In other words, children are being urged to identify with heroes
who symbolize pathological forms of behaviour. The requirement
that the 'miracle worker' should be both on the right side of the
law and yet be able to murder *without guilt feelings* is distinctly

---

[15] S. T. Coleridge, letter to Thomas Poole dated 16 October 1797.

[16] Commercial agent quoted in Jean and Andrew Robertson's introduction to *The
Assault on Childhood*, (Gollancz).

[17] Quoted in William Mellody's *Children's TV* (Yale University Press). Obviously the
situation is worse in America than at present in England but as Stuart Hood pointed out in
a review of *Children's TV* 'Products produced in the States to achieve acculturation to a
society where one can 'shoot to kill without punishment or guilt feelings, are bought and
shown on our screens. Nobody . . . can fail to wonder what effect they have on the
phantasies of the child audience and on their images of life' (*Times Educational
Supplement*, 25 January 1974).

schizoid. It would seem that the young are growing up with heroes or heroines representing infantile levels of response, levels of response before an awareness of the other and a concern for the other has developed. The recent James Bond cult in this country would confirm this analysis — for James Bond celebrates a regression to experience without responsibility, concern or guilt, and sanctifies an identity utterly dependent on consumer artefacts and what, through the copywriters, they have come to symbolize. In this synthetic phantasy, written for success and money, the objects of advertising (cars, jewels, alcohol, clothes, gadgets of all kind, gold) and their pseudo-symbolic references (sexual prowess, speed, mobility, violence, power) interlock. No journey from infancy to maturity is to be found in James Bond, but rather the enclosed ward of the mentally sick.[18] That such a figure became a potent image for selling toys, clothes, cars, cosmetics, and a torrent of consumer trivia, only points us, once again, to the warped phantasies which are manipulated to secure the goals of industrial man.

Man, in industrial society, becomes externalized, becomes preoccupied with objects, machines, techniques — advertising elevates this preoccupation into a theology and a ritual. Children, at a very early age, are compelled to imagine and dream of life as the accumulation of fashionable products. Even dolls are fashioned in the prevailing image:

> She's a really with-it, teen-age doll *always up with the latest fashions,* not only in styles of dress but *also in fashion accessories and hairstyles. Barbie has a costume for every occasion. You choose it — you dress her.* So make friends with Barbie now.[19]

In fact, 'the world of Barbie', to use the phrase of the manufacturers, includes not only hairstyles and dresses, but hundreds of items, from 'Queen beds' to racing cars, from books to 'dream-houses'. Mattels profess to work on the principle of Gillette razor-blades: 'you know, first get them sold on the basic unit, then keep selling them the accessories'.[20]

The actual shape of the doll, with fully developed breasts but attenuated limbs, with gyrating hips, with glossy hair, long eye-lashes and rose-bud lips, derives from and further reinforces the

---

[18] For a lengthy psycho-analytic study of the James Bond cult see David Holbrook's *The Masks of Hate* (Pergamon).

[19] Advertisement for Barbie doll in popular children's comic.

[20] A Barbie 'public-relations' man.

image of female sexuality as projected by advertising and the
commercial pulp of teenage comics. The early play of the child
must fit the demands of machine culture. So much is provided in
the way of visual form, literal detail and accompanying
accessories that very little space remains in which the child can
release his own phantasies and, through projecting them onto his
play objects, give them life. In the last decade, children's toys
have been designed in a progressively more realistic style. (Toy
guns, for example, have been recently used in 'real' hold-ups). It
would seem more than likely that such toys, relating directly to the
prefabricated images of mass-entertainment, instead of fostering
that innate power to create phantasy from within, enforce a
repetition of those stereotyped actions already invented by the
commercial manipulators. Such toys encourage a conformist
mode of play, play in which the dominant values of the external
world are introjected and repeated while the powers to initiate
and invent *from within outwards* atrophy. In this way, the actual
preoccupations of the adult world, as depicted by copywriters
and entertainers, become those of the child. The Advisory Centre
for Education, examining hundreds of letters written to Father
Christmas, concluded that

> The influence of television selling is rather disturbing. Little girls
> seem particularly vulnerable. It is also troubling to see six-year-old
> girls writing to Father Christmas for 'sexy boots' or pop records. A lot
> of girls are asking for 'pureplume' (perfume?) or the latest face
> powder, and a teenage concern with body odour seems to have been
> successfully planted on little girls by mass advertising.[21]

It would, I am sure, be possible to document more fully the
influence of advertising on children. What I have been anxious to
stress is the symbolic dimension of advertising and the way in
which the cultural heritage of true myth and true poetry is being
steadily eroded. I have also been anxious to draw attention to the
general values and assumptions promoted by advertising and
commercial propaganda. Here I find myself largely in agreement
with Jean and Andrew Robertson who have written:

> The communicators are a competitive segment of modern industrial
> society, and right out in front are the trendsetters with their over
> anxiety to shock, jolt, upset or, in their own carefully calculated
> word, stimulate. But what do they stimulate in the young? Kindness,

[21] *The Sunday Times,* 5 December 1971.

generosity, tolerance, sympathy, gentleness? Hardly. These would relate low in the television scale of values as weaknesses.

The qualities most prized are toughness, self-love (as opposed to self-respect), conceit, arrogance, philistinism and anger . . .[22]

The comment would seem to apply particularly to the advertisements and entertainment directed at children. Elsewhere, as I have indicated, we often find a spurious appeal to creative emotions, love, sympathy and tenderness. It would seem to me that both appeals, whether to the low or the high, are equally dangerous for while one urges into action crude and destructive forms of behaviour, the other dilutes, parodies and destroys the deeper aspirations of man.

I have presented in broad outline the case against advertising conceived as a symbolic system. However, there is nothing particularly new in the general drift of my argument. The earliest movements towards an imaginative form of English teaching were concerned to restrict questionable adult influences on the child. In 1920, Dorothy Owen wrote:

The sweeping clear their minds of all prejudice, second-hand opinions, pre-conceived notions, that is the hard task . . . Before ever we can get children to express themselves we must sweep their minds clear, remove the darkened spectacles, and turn their eyes toward the direct vision. Once they are freed from the restraint of opinion they can learn to tell us what they see.[23]

For Dorothy Owen, the child, at the beginning of the twentieth century, had not the realization of what its experiences were. As it grew, so the garb of preconceived opinion was tightly wound round its senses. Dorothy Owen doesn't directly relate this dimming of individual experience to the growing network of mass communications, but in 1933 Denys Thompson and F. R. Leavis made the connection explicit:

Those who in school are offered (perhaps) the beginnings of education in taste are exposed, out of school, to the competing exploitation of the cheapest emotional responses; films, newspapers, publicity in all its forms, commercially-catered fiction, all offer satisfaction at the lowest level, and inculcate the choosing of the most immediate pleasure, got with the least effort . . .

---

[22] Jean and Andrew Robertson in their Introduction to *The Assault on Childhood* (Gollancz).

[23] Dorothy Owen, *The Child Vision* (Manchester University Press).

The school-training of literary taste does indeed look a forlorn enterprise.[24]

Nearly forty years later, Richard Hoggart in his Reith Lectures (1971) was to make a similar condemnation:

You look over a sad and virtually world-wide panorama of the media in chains: in chains to the fooling and narrowing purposes of selling: in chains to the narrowing and stifling purposes of the national powers-that-be and their insistent fixed picture of what their culture is and shall be.

Even more recently, in *The Imagery of Power* (1972),[25] Fred Inglis has shown how the counterfeit symbolic system of advertising exists to hide the latent contradiction between mass-production and growth economics, for, in a society, where the *actual* necessities of life can be provided easily for all, there exists a historically unique opportunity to create the sane society, where the creative, aesthetic and philosophical energies of man could be widely and harmoniously cultivated. In this light, advertising can be understood as a gigantic endeavour to close the circle against the pressing alternatives for man's development.

But how, in practical terms, can the English teacher help to break open the circle so that creative vision and intellectual speculation can assert their liberating influence on life? I would suggest he has the four following responsibilities:

1. To create, in contrast, a truly creative and honest use of language and symbol as described in Chapter 3.
2. To encourage his pupils, through the proper study of literature, to become aware of cultural and moral ideals.
3. To consider ways in which the school could be transformed into a cultural centre for the surrounding community as suggested in Chapter 9.
4. To foster in his pupils a critical attitude towards publicity, advertising and propaganda.

In our society these are exacting responsibilities. Many adolescents are so identified with the images cast by the media, that they positively do not wish to see that they are being cynically manipulated, or, if they do see, do not care. Yet their responses only italicize our responsibilities. What, then, can the teacher do in the classroom?

[24] F. R. Leavis & Denys Thompson, *Culture and Environment* (Chatto & Windus).
[25] Inglis, *The Imagery of Power* (Heinemann Educational Books).

II

How can the teacher encourage his pupils to be critical of advertising in a society decorated so insistently and so constantly by the glamour and glory of advertising? Any detailed examination of persuasion requires the understanding of a number of abstract concepts and, for this reason, such study is best reserved for fourth and fifth forms in the secondary school. Our general aim must be to promote sensitive and personal reflection on all the issues raised by commercial propaganda. Ideally, we would like each individual in the class to be able to analyse *any* advertisement, to be able to ask both '*What* is this particular advertisement suggesting, stating, symbolizing?' and '*How* is it doing it'; and then to know ways in which he can set about answering such questions. Furthermore we should hope that each pupil, before leaving school, has had an opportunity to reflect on the proper place of advertising in society, to have considered, through reading, research, writing and discussion, such questions as: Why do advertisements exist? How much do they cost? Who pays for them? Are they necessary? Do they control, in any way, the content of ITV, of magazines, of newspapers? Do they propagate false values and false expectations? Do they destroy the meaning of words? And are they closed to public scrutiny and criticism?

For a variety of reasons the English teacher will find it difficult to discover an excellent textbook on advertising.[26] He will, therefore, have to rely, to a large extent, on his own resources, duplicating his own selection of advertisements and quotations. I offer the following outline of a course on advertising as one possible way of initiating and developing the habits of discrimination and criticism. I believe that, because the subject matter is so vast and yet so close to us, it is important for the teacher to introduce both conceptual tools and practical

[26] One of the reasons for the absence of good textbooks on advertising is that many important companies will not allow their advertisements to be reproduced in any critical context. As I write, I have two letters on my desk, one refusing to allow permission for a cigarette advertisement to be reproduced, the other, an advertisement for gin. The letter from Rothmans Limited reads: 'I am afraid that we cannot give our permission for the reproduction of our advertisement. There are several reasons for our policy in this matter. We would prefer not to have advertisements for our products drawn to the attention of young people specifically. More generally, we should be reluctant to have our advertisements singled out for specific criticism in a context where we could obviously have no right of reply.' For his own reading, however, the teacher will find Fred Inglis' *The Imagery of Power* and Raymond Williams' *Communications* invaluable.

exercises. Without techniques for effective analysis and comparison, there is a danger that classroom discussion will become vague and deteriorate to the level of rhetorical assertion (I think that . . .) and counter-assertion (Well, I don't . . .). Our aim should be to make such assertions informed and intelligent, whether we personally agree with them or not. The best way to secure considered judgements on immediate and somewhat controversial matters is not only to present the class with specific problems but also to introduce various ways in which they can be quietly and rigorously examined.

Here, then, in schematic form, is a possible course on advertising aiming to foster an alert discrimination towards the commercial media.

Work can begin with the class being given sheets, prepared by the teacher, recording a series of juxtaposed and mostly contradictory comments and, if possible, images. In discussing and attempting to clarify the nature of the confusions involved, the class, perhaps working in small groups, will inevitably become aware, often for the first time, of the powers and intentions of mass advertising.

Here are three selections of the sort of juxtapositions I have in mind.

1. *TOBACCO*

   (a) The evidence is now incontrovertible that the cigarette is the main cause of the present epidemic of lung cancer, the steady toll of which is comparable in its magnitude with that of such infections of the past as cholera, typhoid, and tuberculosis. Cigarette smoking is also a major cause of chronic bronchitis and emphysema, with its years of distressing breathlessness and its ultimately high mortality. It is a major contributory factor in the increasing death-rate from coronary thrombosis, as well as in the diffuse arterial degeneration that gradually closes the arteries of the lower limbs and characteristically makes walking at first agonisingly painful and ultimately impossible.[27]

   (b) St Moritz has a ring of luxury about it longer, richer, cooler.

      Now in King Size
      The Extra Mild cigarettes you can *taste*

[27] Henry Miller in *The Listener*, 14 January 1971.

John Player Special
Created and perfected to be the best Virginia cigarette in the world.

A long moment of pleasure.

(c) 'Now the question of smoking and its injury to health is that if you smoke to excess, it is bad for your health, exactly the same as if you drink to excess, if you eat to excess, if you eat sweets to excess, and so on. And if you're going to let Aunty Government or anybody else interfere [with advertising cigarettes] we're going to have a very drab dull life. I think that it is one of the minor vices . . .'[28] (Note the source)

2. TRUTH?

(a) STOP THE OTHER WOMAN STARTING
However happily the marriage starts it always settles down . . . Colour yourself back to your old self. With Casual. Before the other woman comes along.[29]

(b) BRITISH HUSBANDS
CARE LESS
FOR THEIR WIVES
THAN AMERICAN
OR CONTINENTAL
HUSBANDS
American and Continental husbands are all in favour of liberating their wives from the kitchen sink. Not so the British.[30]

(c) A copywriter writes in two dimensions. His technical triumph is to make what is one-sided seem round . . . He has to cook with sugar instead of salt, draw with all light and no shadow, yet somehow make the result both engaging and convincing.[31]

(d) When public promises are of such a character that things do *not* happen as predicted—when, after we have done as we were told, the peace in the soul has not been found, the taxes have not been reduced, the boy friend has not returned, there is disappointment. Such disappointments may be trivial or grave; in any event they are so common that we do not even bother to complain about some of them. They are, nevertheless, all serious in their implications. Each of them serves, in greater or less

[28] Jack Wynne-Williams, President of the Advertising Association, on *Its Your line* (BBC).
[29] From advertisement for *Casual*.
[30] From advertisement for *Colstons*.
[31] From *Copywriting as a Career* (The Advertising Creative Circle).

degree, to break down that mutual trust that makes co-operation possible and knits people together into a society.

Every one of us there who utters a public promise is morally obliged to be as certain as he can that he is arousing no false expectations. Politicians promising the immediate abolition of poverty, national advertisers suggesting that tottering marriages can be restored to bliss by a change in the brand of laundry detergent used in the family, newspapers threatening the collapse of the nation if the party they favour is not elected—all such utterers of nonsense are, for the reasons stated, menaces to the social order. It does not matter much whether such promises are uttered in ignorance and error or with conscious intent to deceive, because the disappointments they cause are all similarly destructive of mutual trust among human beings.[32]

3. RICH AND POOR?

(a) We must accelerate obsolescence . . .
It is our job to make women unhappy with what they have.[33]

(b) Save £5, get £2 free
            —and easy!
If the thought of free money appeals to you, read on.[34]

(c) Future generations may well marvel that in our day science and technology could transform so much in the world but still not guarantee decent life for its hungry millions.

Mass hunger is something that has hardly changed. War, poverty and exploitation are still the greatest enemies of the human race, bringing death, mutilation, hunger and disease to countless millions who, even without war, are facing starvation. Indeed, poverty and hunger have increased in the so-called 'third world' today—those countries in Asia, Africa, Latin America and the Caribbean which, from the economic standpoint, are under-developed in comparison to the rest of the world and which comprise over half the total world population.[35]

(d) Well over 90% of the world's metals are being used by less than a third of its population. The rich are getting richer on the resources that come, very often, from the poor.[36]

---

[32] I have simplified the quotation from Hayakawa's *Language in Thought and Action* (George Allen & Unwin). The main change I have made is to substitute his phrase 'directive utterances' for 'public promises'.

[33] Earl Puckett, Chairman of Allied Stores Co-operation.

[34] From National Savings Advertisement.

[35] Idris Cox in *The Hungry Half* (Lawrence & Wishart).

[36] Nigel Hawkes, *Daily Telegraph Colour Supplement*, 3 December 1971.

These quotations, and others like them, perhaps reproduced with a few guiding questions, will inevitably draw attention to the general purposes of advertising and its relation to our affluent society. The field of advertising now opened up, needs studying in closer detail. Certain distinctions, definitions, and tasks need introducing. It is, perhaps, important, in the first place, to divide the various forms of advertising into the following groups:

CLASSIFIED ADVERTISING
This advertising, generally printed in columns, classified under various headings e.g. Wanted, For Sale, Miscellaneous. Classified advertising differs from paper to paper. A classified advertisement costs more in a big national paper than in a small local paper. In both cases, however, the majority of people could afford, if they so wished, to pay for advertisement space. In fact, many people do use classified advertisements, particularly in local papers, to sell and buy things as well as to formally announce important events like births, marriages, and deaths.

DISPLAY ADVERTISING
Display advertising is advertising which uses considerable space to attractively present products and commercial messages. Space in papers for display advertising, in contrast to classified advertising, is extremely expensive. A full page in *The News of the World* can cost in the region of £4,400. It is obvious that advertising so expensive to procure is not open to the majority of individuals or to small or medium-sized businesses.

OTHER FORMS OF ADVERTISING
1. Commercial radio.
2. Commercial television.
3. Exhibitions (e.g. Motor Show).
4. Mail Orders and Circulars.
5. Door to door salesmanship.
6. Packaging[37] (not all packaging—some is necessary for reasons of hygiene).
7. Brochures. 'Free' Pamphlets. 'Educational' Films.
8. Features in Papers and magazines (e.g. supplements on Holidays and fashions. These can look like part of the publication but are little more than advertisements in disguise

---

[37] Packaging is, in fact, a very important form of advertising. In 1970, £670 million was spent on packaging whereas £520 million was spent on direct advertising.

and are produced to attract advertisements to the publications).
9. Public Hoardings.

The important distinction to draw in any discussion about the forms of advertising is the one between those which are open to the general public and those which, because of the expense involved, are closed to all except the large and wealthy firms and corporations (sixty seconds on Thames Television, after seven o'clock, for example, will cost about £3,200).[38] While the class can examine and discuss the function and style of classified advertisements, the study will obviously concentrate on the commercial forms of advertising. To begin such work it is useful to introduce a number of simple linguistic definitions as follows:

A STATEMENT
A statement is a description of the world which can be checked and shown to be true or false.

Thus: 'WILLS IMPERIAL TOBACCO IS ONE OF THE WEALTHIEST INDUSTRIES IN BRITAIN' or 'Rothman's is an American Tobacco firm', are both Statements — which could be checked and found (at least at the date of publication) to be true.

A JUDGEMENT
A judgement is an expression of a personal viewpoint concerning the world.

Thus: 'WILLS TOBACCO IS THE FINEST TOBACCO IN THE WORLD' or 'Rothman's have a smooth satisfying flavour', are both judgements — with which you may agree or disagree.

These two distinctions provide useful tools for the examination of some advertisements. The class could be given a list of quotations from advertisements and asked to decide whether they form statements or judgements. They could then be asked whether they agree or disagree with the judgements as well as where they could check the reliability or unreliability of the statements. Here is one possible list:

1. Cow & Gate. For contented Sunday afternoons.
2. There's nowhere like Butlin's for dad.
3. The stainless steel Parker 61. £3.15.
4. Packets carry a government health warning.

[38] For further information about the cost of advertising see Fred Inglis' *The Imagery of Power*, op. cit.

5. With Persil Automatic your front loader will do a better job.
6. Kenwood gives you more time.
7. The morning after should be just as beautiful as the night before. Pure, clean Cossack vodka.
8. You can buy this car for under £1,500.
9. There ought to be a lot more Simca 1100's on British roads.
10. Written with great honesty and frankness, lavishly illustrated with uninhibited photographs . . .
11. Ekco Hostess Cabinet. Only £16.95.

Some advertisements do easily divide into statements and judgements. Thus, for example, one advertisement's headline, 'The greatest most superb offer of all times', is clearly a judgement, while the detail in smaller print 'Price £1 from your nearest TV dealer' is clearly a statement. However, many advertisements do not break into these divisions, for, as we have seen, they employ a poetic language, a language of suggestion and decoration and there the concept of associative language needs introducing.

ASSOCIATIVE LANGUAGE
Associate language is language which has the power to conjure up in the mind various sensations, feelings, and memories. It is used by copywriters because they hope the reader or viewer will connect the pleasant associations aroused (through word and picture) to a particular product and brand name.

An examination of brand names quickly reveals to the class the meaning of the term 'associative'. Why, they could be asked, were the following names selected by the giant companies?:

Austin, Princess, Avenger, Triumph, Escapade, Brut, Embassy, Piccadilly, King, Country Maid, Mother's Pride, Sunblest, Champion, Gold Blend.

It is not difficult to see that these words have been selected not for their accuracy but for their associative powers. It is the same with many glossy advertisements e.g. 'A nightclub of legs. Bare Thigh. Flower Petal' and 'The gleaming sheen of pearl. The soft dew — bright highlights. The lustre . . . Pearly illusion'. It is now possible for the class to apply the concepts of judgement, statement and association in a systematic examination of specific advertisements. The following task could be set:

Cut out a number of advertisements and examine the language.
Comment on the statements and judgements and describe the nature of the persuasion.

It could also be pointed out that many pictures work in a similar fashion. Some pictures give an accurate image of the product (rather like a statement). Others place the product in a particular setting, implying that a certain style of living accompanies the object (in the manner of many advertising judgements). Others dispense with the product and evoke various ecstatic sensations (in the manner of associations). With the help of these distinctions[39] the class can be asked to analyse the visual content of advertisements.

With a reasonably able class the abuse of concepts in advertising could now be broached. The following quotations, concerning political propaganda, might be used to open up the discussion:

> A Senator, distinguished, powerful, an astute leader with surpassing skill in political management, told me that Americanism was to be this year's campaign issue. When I asked him what Americanism meant, he said he did not know, but that it was a damned good word with which to carry an election.[40]

First politician

> Ancient institutions and modern improvements might form a good slogan.

Second politician

> Ameliorations is the better word; ameliorations. Nobody knows exactly what it means.[41]

> Defenceless villages are bombarded from the air, the inhabitants driven out into the countryside, the cattle machine-gunned, the huts set on fire with incendiary bullets: this is called pacification. Millions of peasants are robbed of their farms and set trudging along the roads with no more than they can carry: this is called transfer of population or rectification of frontiers. People are imprisoned for years without trials or shot in the back of the neck or sent to die of scurvy in Arctic lumber camps: this is called elimination of unreliable elements.[42]

Following a discussion of these passages, practical work might move to (a) a listing of possible euphemisms for uncomfortable

---

[39] With an able 5th form or 6th form the distinction between *sign* (having an exact reference) and *symbol* (expressing a multiplicity of feelings and meanings) could also be introduced here.

[40] Stuart Chase in *The Tyranny of Words* (Methuen).

[41] Adapted from a conversation in Disraeli's *Coningsby*.

[42] George Orwell in *Politics and the English Language*.

terms such as death, poverty, killing, etc, (b) an examination of
Estate Agents' hand-outs, and (c) the use and abuse of concepts in
advertising. Some of the following examples could be taken, with
particular attention being drawn to the words in italics.

1. Its a *Natural,* Rothman's Masters: a cigarette with the *natural*
   balance of filter and flavour.
2. The car that *nature* intended.
3. *Civilised* Stereo by HMV.
4. *Independence Day* is the day you first switch on your Shell-Mex
   and BP Central Heating.
5. A way to give to *charity* which doesn't cost you a penny.
6. 4,000 unemployed in firm's *rationalisation* scheme.
7. Women's *Liberation*—Colston's Dishwasher.
8. The Great Wash Up *Revolution's* overdue. Fill in the coupon—
9. *Revolutionary* bullworker. Builds muscles many times faster than
   conventional techniques.
10. *Free:* with every gallon of petrol.
11. And if after closing time, your man invites a crowd of his friends
    back for supper, he knows he'll have to make it himself unless he
    remembers to bring home a few bottles of Guinness for you too.
    It's what you might call *progress.* We're in favour of it.
12. The *pure* substitute.

Having introduced a number of important concepts and
having applied them to specific advertisements, we might well
conclude the first part of the course with the following tasks:

1. Write a simple classified advertisement describing the product
   through a series of useful statements.
2. Design a display advertisement for the same product with a
   minimum of statements and a maximum of judgements.
3. Design another advertisement which dispenses with both
   statements and judgements and relies on associations and the
   brand name for its affect.

   (Comment on the problems and difficulties involved. How did
   you decide on the words and images? What audience did you
   have in mind? What sort of magazine or paper would your
   advertisement tend to fit?)
4. Rework your advertisements with a different audience in mind.

The object of the remaining work is to analyse the less obvious
impact of advertising on human communications. Here the
relation between the methods of advertising and the methods for
promoting mass-entertainment could be examined, with the

language of the disc jockey, the pop star,[43] and the teenage magazine being carefully studied. Another task could be to compare the methods of political propaganda to the methods of commercial persuasion. (The teacher will find some of the scripts of President Nixon's commercials in *The Selling of the President*).[44] Here, however, I would like to briefly outline ways in which one can reveal the influence advertising exerts on contemporary newspapers and magazines. With an able class the following quotations could be read out and discussed.

1. Though newspapers have carried advertisements for 200 years, it is only in the last half century that they have become dependant on them for their very existence. The press is generally assumed to wield great power, but its power is more economic than political or even sociological. Most newspapers make money and in the past some have made much more than they do these days; they are business enterprises, usually belonging to big and widely diversified groups. But they contradict the basic law of business by choosing to sell at a loss. Their artificially depressed price enables them to sustain circulations big enough to attract advertisers, and the revenue from actual sales is of secondary importance![45]

2. In so far as the media are controlled by commercial interests, then the management and presentation of knowledge will inevitably be loaded with various implications. Nor can we have much doubt that the first intention of a newspaper or of commercial television is to gain advertising revenue.

All newspapers, like ITV and magazines, sustain their readership in the terms which their main commercial sponsors can accept.[46]

3. It is difficult, in the popular papers to separate, at first glance, the news and advertisement photographs, while in layout and topography there is often no distinction between advertising and editorial material. It is then not possible to separate advertising from the general effect of the paper. It is not an isolated item, a kind of support cast, but part of the total communication. The most extreme development of this kind is in the women's magazines, where it is

---

[43] According to the business magazine *The Director* the pop stars 'are the new aristocracy. They provide the social leadership for their generation and, more obviously, they have accumulated great wealth . . . yes industry and the financial establishment have been slow to get to grips with *this novel and rapid way of generating enormous inflows of cash*' (May 1974). My italics.
For a developed criticism of pop music see Charles Parker's essay *The Manipulated Ritual* in *The Black Rainbow* (Heinemann Education Books).

[44] Joe McGinniss, *The Selling of the President* (André Deutsch).

[45] Denis Thomas in *The Visible Persuaders* (Hutchinson).

[46] Fred Inglis in *The Imagery of Power* (Heinemann Educational Books).

often difficult, without close inspection, to identify an advertisement, and where the verbal and visual styles combine with the similarity of interests to produce a single overall effect. Another relevant case is the advertising supplement, in which apparently independent editorial treatment of products and services is printed alongside direct advertisement in a planned way.[47]

4. Whole passages from stories in the women's magazines could often be lifted straight from the advertisement pages. They use the same verbal symbols for domesticity, married love, the glamour of faraway places, and the same tone of voice — friendly, sensible, with an admixture of what agency copy-writers would recognise as sincere-type phraseology.[48]

When some of the more difficult concepts in these passages have been elucidated and their general meaning understood, the following practical studies could be made.

1. *An examination of a cross-section of newspapers with the aid of the following questions:*

(a) What percentage of the paper is made up of advertisements?
(b) How have the advertisements been placed in the newspapers?
(c) Why have they been placed in this way?
(d) What revenue would the paper receive from all the advertisements?
(e) Has any of the editorial matter been influenced by the language of advertising?
(f) How do the advertisements relate to the readers of the paper?

2. *An examination of a colour supplement with the aid of the following questions:*

(a) What percentage of the supplement is made up of advertising?
(b) What percentage is made up with editorial material?
(c) What sort of products are being advertised? Why?
(d) How much of the editorial material resembles in content or presentation the advertising?
(e) Why do colour supplements exist?

3. *A similar examination of a cross-section of adolescents' and women's magazines with these additional questions:*

(a) How many examples of 'sincere-type phraseology' can you find?
(b) How true is the comment that the stories and advertisements are almost the same?

[47] Raymond Williams in *Communications* (Penguin).
[48] Denis Thomas in *The Visible Persuaders* (Hutchinson).

(c) How many articles seem to have been written to draw advertising?

If some of the class are a little uncertain about how the language of advertising can come to influence the way our news is presented, particularly the 'popular' papers, the editorial below, taken from *The Mirror*, should leave few doubts on the issue. Indeed, the passage could be duplicated and the class asked to pinpoint the words, phrases and sentences which have been taken over from the copywriter:

> You have to be a real sour square not to love the nutty, noisy, happy, handsome Beatles.
> If they don't sweep your blues away — brother, you're a lost cause. If they don't put a beat in your feet — sister, you're not living.
> How refreshing to see these rumbustious young Beatles take a middle-aged Royal Variety Performance audience by the scruff of their necks and have them beatling like teenagers.
> Fact is that Beatle People are everywhere. From Wapping to Windsor. Aged seven to seventy. And it's plain to see why these four energetic, cheeky lads from Liverpool go down so big.
> They're young, new. They're high-spirited, cheerful. What a change from the self-pitying moaners crooning their love-lorn tunes from the tortured shallows of lukewarm hearts.
> The Beatles are whacky. They wear their hair like a mop — but it's WASHED, it's super clean. So is their fresh young set. They don't have to rely on off-colour jokes about homos for their fun.
> Youngsters like the Beatles — and Cliff Richard and the Shadows — are doing a good turn for show business — and the rest of us — with their new sounds, new looks.
> GOOD LUCK, BEATLES![49]

The most superficial analysis of *The Mirror* and 'the full of fun *Sun*' would expose two 'newspapers' in which the necessary distinctions between advertising, entertainment and information have been all but obliterated. 'In so far as the media are controlled by commercial interests, then the management and presentation of knowledge will inevitably be loaded with various implications'. At the end of the course, the class could discuss the alternatives to a press sponsored by commerce.[50] Finally, they

[49] *Daily Mirror* Editorial, November 1963.

[50] Looking at newspapers from the perspective of advertising does not, of course, give a complete picture of the press today. At a later point, the teacher might decide to balance the portrait by beginning a detailed study of contemporary newspapers. Here the teacher would find Ian Robinson's vigorous attack on *The Times* in *The Survival of English* (Cambridge University Press) invaluable.

could return to consider in more detail, the broad issues with which they began.

The course I have outlined may seem slanted to one end. In defense, I would argue that our pupils, through the persuasive forces of the media, are encouraged always to see another view, a conformist view wholly in the interests of the prevailing money élites. The purpose of an effective course on advertising (and many, to judge from existing textbooks, are ineffective) is to open up the closed communications of the copywriters so that their methods and claims can be calmly and intelligently assessed. In this way we provide each pupil with the means, if he so wishes, to resist the emotional pressures of the propagandists. It would seem to me axiomatic that education, dedicated to the development of the whole man, has every right to provide the means for such resistance. As Vance Packard claimed:

> The unorganized consumer must resist blind conformity to the group and to the commercial persuader. Education is central to his resistance.[51]

In the first part of this essay I suggested that the methods and forms of advertising had spilt over their commercial boundaries and had become, in many instances, those of the artist and writer. First the American painter, then the European, stealing the pseudo-imagery of the copywriters, came to celebrate the banal. Films and novels became progressively more sensational in subject matter and, to secure commercial success, came to depend on all manner of promotional stunts and media puffs. In short, I hope to have shown how, under the powers exerted by a highly organized and amoral commercialism, there was a danger that art, in its widest sense, was being robbed of both its creative and critical functions. Furthermore there was a danger that others, reacting against the cant and hypocrisy of commercialized culture, would retreat into wilful obscurity or the black comforts of intellectual nihilism. It is this latter response and its bearing on the teaching of contemporary literature that I wish now to analyse.

[51] Vance Packard in *The Waste Makers* (Longman).

FIVE

Contemporary Literature and the

Problems of Nihilism

Unless there is somewhere an intelligent critical attitude against which the writer can measure himself . . . one of the chief requirements for good literature is wanting . . . The author degenerates.

Henry S. Canby

We should not expose our private paranoia to the world, but seek to master it in art and through art. The alternative is an unrestrained exposure of mental conflicts or mental confusion that in terms of visual or poetic form is aesthetic nihilism.

Herbert Read

I

It must be one of our tasks in the sixth forms and in Colleges of Education to introduce our students to modern and contemporary literature. This is not an easy matter. Much of modern literature is obscure, private in its own references and symbols, a desperate endeavour to create some semblance of pattern before darkness falls. Even more disturbing is the fact that the dominant tone of contemporary literature is black, even nihilistic, portraying, as often as not, a universe whirling through the vacuum of space without purpose and without hope. There is a danger, perhaps, that we offer, at an impressionable age, and at an age disposed towards social idealism, a bleak and remorseless vision of life stripped of its diversities, beauties and possibilities. In presenting contemporary literature, we could, unwittingly, be responsible for disseminating a philosophy of ultimate helplessness, encouraging our students to interpret their experience through the single category of futility.

Yet, at the same time, we have a responsibility to see that our students are aware of contemporary literature, for criticism, which is unable to confront and examine the present moment, is also powerless to effectively evaluate the past. T. S. Eliot claimed:

> The rudiment of criticism is the ability to select a good poem and reject a bad poem: and its most severe test is of its ability to select a good new poem, to respond properly to a new situation.[1]

We must, therefore, be ready to respond properly, with due sensibility and due discrimination, to new developments in contemporary literature and encourage our students to do likewise. Certainly, any course in contemporary literature must be something more than a passive exposure to those fashionable works so constantly promulgated by the London circuit of intellectuals and journalists. It is, also, vital that our students have some general understanding of the historical context in which many of the more questionable manifestations of the arts need to be placed. We may live by moving forward, but only comprehend by looking backwards . . .

II

For the last three centuries or so, Western man has devoted the best portion of his intellectual and spiritual energies to the general accumulation of scientific knowledge and the successive application of that knowledge to procure material abundance, physical comfort and secular well-being. At the centre of this ambition to have knowledge and power over objects[2] was locked a philosophy which gave absolute assent only to those things which could be handled, organized, tabulated and tested. Truth and Fact came to be synonymous. From the Renaissance onwards, according to Susanne Langer:

> Knowledge from sensory experience was deemed the only knowledge that carried any affidavit of truth: for truth came to be identified, for all vigorous minds, with empirical fact.[3]

Facts become more real than values, techniques more treasured than meanings, experimentation more valued than speculation. Under the sway of scientific assumptions and the fascinations of mechanical power (of speed and mobility), the development of

---

[1] T. S. Eliot in *The Use of Poetry and the Use of Criticism* (Faber & Faber).
[2] It was the empiricist Francis Bacon who wrote about putting Nature 'on the rack' and to examine her 'with levers and screws'. Domination has always been an important element in Western Science.
[3] Susanne Langer, *Philosophy in a New Key* (Mentor Books).

the inward man, through the powers of religion and culture, came to be disregarded and, finally, all but denied. 'Man', proclaimed William Blake, rebelling against the empiricism of Locke and Newton, 'has closed himself up till he sees all things through narrow chinks of his cavern'. As technical skill and knowledge of objects expanded, so did the more primitive and mythopoeic forms of perception and imagination contract. The poets were aware, at a very early point in industrial and scientific development, that the Progress promised and proclaimed by the Enlightenment was a progress towards a future in which the higher forms of understanding, as symbolized in the Arts, would have little chance to exist.

In the middle of the nineteenth century Matthew Arnold wrote:

> The idea of perfection as an inward condition of the mind and spirit is at variance with the mechanical and material civilization with us.[4]

In our own century, Yeats classified the movement towards empirical fact and psychological control[5] as an inexorable swing away from the inner self:

> At the present moment the life gyre is sweeping outwards . . . all our scientific, democratic, fact-accumulating civilization belongs to the outward gyre.[6]

Heterogeneous civilization, as I will try to show in the final chapter of this book, has no place for culture, for civilization is mechanical and gazes outwards while culture is organic and directs its attention inwards towards the unchanging centre.

The Romantics were the first to assert this truth on a sublime scale. Against mechanism, they asserted the unifying power of the imagination on which the human world, in all its complexity, depends.

> O Lady! we receive but what we give,
> And in our life alone does Nature live:

[4] Matthew Arnold, *Culture and Anarchy*.

[5] This desire to control has only recently been examined and criticized. In *Life Against Death* Norman Brown writes, 'What is being probed, and found to be in some sense morbid, is not knowledge as such, but the unconscious schemata governing the pursuit of knowledge in modern civilization—specifically the aim of possession or mastery over objects, and the principle of economizing in the means. And the morbidity imputed to these schemata amounts to this: possessive mastery over nature and rigorously economical thinking are partial impulses in the human being which in modern civilizations have become tyrant organizers of the whole of human life'. See also *The Cult of the Fact* by Liam Hudson (Jonathan Cape) and *Science and Belief* by Christopher Small (*Tract* 8).

[6] W. B. Yeats, *A Vision* (Macmillan).

Ours is her wedding garment, ours her shroud!
And should we ought behold of higher worth,
Than that inanimate cold world allowed
To the poor loveless ever-anxious crowd,
Ah! from the soul itself must issue forth
A light, a glory, a fair luminous cloud
Enveloping the earth —
And from the soul itself must there be sent
A sweet and potent voice, of its own birth,
Of all sweet sounds the life and element.

In this stanza of *Ode to Dejection* Coleridge is celebrating imagination as that faculty through which we perceive and recreate the world. For Coleridge, as for Blake who declared 'Where man is not, nature is barren', the beauty and meaning we find in the universe is largely projected by our own powers of consciousness. It is 'the soul' which 'enveloping the earth' finds itself reflected in what it admires. In *Frost at Midnight* Coleridge describes the human mind as 'the idling spirit . . . every where/Echo or mirror seeking of itself'. Without this power *to envelope what is outside of us with what is within us,* the universe becomes, as Coleridge declares, 'inanimate' and 'cold'. This is one of the most important insights of the Romantic movement. In the paintings of Samuel Palmer the fair luminous cloud envelopes the landscapes so that we see both the natural objects of landscape and, at the same instant, their visionary forms. While Palmer's paintings take us out in the known corners and hummocks of the English countryside, they also present a haunted domain which takes us, strangely, deep into our own psyches.

The Romantic rebellion was not only, in its highest manifestations, a sublime assertion of man's creative intelligence, but, as I wish to show in more detail in Chapter 8, it also provided an indispensable counterpoint to a social system in which the subjective dimension of existence was in danger of being erased. Yet the isolation of the Romantics from the mainstream of intellectual life fostered, inevitably, feelings of anxiety, persecution, guilt, paranoia and a general uncertainty. In the lives, for example, of Coleridge, Blake, Van Gogh and D. H. Lawrence we can occasionally glimpse the shadowed underside of Romanticism. And as the positive aspirations of the movement withered, so, in our own century, the darker and chaotic feelings tended to occupy the centre of the stage. Indeed, in the last few decades, the arts have become increasingly irrational, hostile both to coherent meaning and articulate feeling. In some cases, the bridges between artist and audience, between shared values and personal vision, between the conscious and the unconscious, have been torn down and, in their place, an inaccessible underground of absurdity and perversion established. The critic A. Alvarez has declared:

> Whether it encourages the criminal life or not, the aim of the artist is to encourage the psychopath within himself.[7]

It may be possible that in such a way the arts will secure their own obscure domain but only at the expense of mangling that essential web of coherent symbolism which draws man and man together to enhance and quicken the rhythm of life.

Lewis Mumford has described the present condition of the international arts as follows:

> From the normally creative minds of poets and artists have come an explosion of anti-life in images that correspond to the outbursts of delinquency and criminality that haunt our daily affairs and that collectively, actually threaten the existence of mankind.
>
> By a total inversion of human values, the favored leaders and mentors of our age prefer disease to health, pornography to potent sexual experience, debasement to development.[8]

Such an account, describing the inversion of human values, returns us to our starting point about the danger, in studying contemporary literature, of disseminating a philosophy of ultimate futility. How can this be avoided? It is, I believe, important for the student to be offered some sort of map — such as the one I have briefly outlined in this section and to which I return, again and again, in these essays — so that he doesn't merely acquiesce to individual works but is able actively to interpret them through an awareness of values, developments and possibilities. Much that is nihilistic in contemporary art can be understood, if not endorsed, through an analysis of the position of the artist in industrial society. The student, who has a range of references and a knowledge of past culture, is equipped to meet the new with a critical intelligence and seminal energies. He is

---

[7] A. Alvarez in *American After-thoughts* (*Encounter,* June 1965).

[8] Lewis Mumford in *Interpretations and Forecasts* (Secker and Warburg).

free from being tyrannized by the fashionable, the trivial and the pretentious.[9]

I want now to critically examine the state of English poetry which, since the Second World War, in contrast to the broad current I have described, has tended to keep away from the flood waters, only to paddle in shallow and somewhat stagnant pools.

III

Since the Second World War the dominant tone of English poetry has been urbane. It is as if, after the seminal work of Eliot, Joyce, Pound and Yeats, the poets moved out to the suburbs choosing for their subject matter the tedious repetitions of domestic life under the Welfare State, lightened only by the occasional wedding. Like a man meticulously adjusting his tie before his own death, so the poets in English polished their unambitious lines, blind to the vast issues posed by their own moribund civilization. *Not with a bang but with a whimper* . . .

Two recent books of poetry, R. S. Thomas' *H'm* and Ted Hughes' *Crow,* have courageously attempted to move beyond the narrowly fenced backwaters of English poetry. Both books have failings, serious failings, as I hope to show, but they do reveal a determination to fashion a new style of poetry, a poetry returning to its dark origins in myth and magic, ritual and chant, while remaining wholly modern in reference. This burrowing back to primeval sources can be felt at once in the rhythms of their language. The following lines are taken from the opening poem in *H'm:*

> God looked at space and I appeared
> Rubbing my eyes at what I saw
> The earth smoked, no birds sang;
> There were no footprints on the beaches
> Of the hot sea, no creatures in it.
> God spoke. I hid myself in the side
> of the mountain.

These lines are taken from one of the concluding poems in *Crow:*

> Water wanted to live
> It went to the sun it came weeping back
> Water wanted to live

[9] Of course, we must also encourage our students to read the best of what is being written, e.g. the work of David Jones, George MacKay Brown, Alexander Solzhenitsyn, Charles Tomlinson, Chinua Achebe.

It went to the trees they burned it came weeping back
Water wanted to live
It went to the flowers they crumpled it came weeping
                                                    back.

I quote these short excerpts only to show the free-ranging style
of the poetry, its immediacy, its vastness. The lines from Ted
Hughes possess, although the emotion is bitter, the same sort of
resonance as one finds in the Psalms, in religious litanies, in
primitive chants. The words take us beyond their obvious and
conventional references into primordial worlds inhabited by
warring energies. At the beginning of R. S. Thomas' poem, we
are presented with the creation of man and at the end, as Adam
and Eve move forward 'to meet the Machine', we sense imminent
discord and disaster. Both poems work in the manner of myth and
yet without any archaicism of language, without any academic
trappings. The two books represent a powerful attempt to reclaim
the great metaphysical issues of traditional poetry, which, since
the Second World War, under the influence of the academic and
urbane poets, had seemed beyond the reach of contemporary
imagination. Furthermore, the recent poetry of Thomas and
Hughes does not evade the burden of industrial experience, but
attempts, through broad imaginative gestures, to express its
nature and influence. R. S. Thomas writes:

> Knowledge is power;
> The old oracle
> Has not changed. The nucleus
> In the atom awaits
> Our bidding. Come forth,
> We cry, and the dust spreads
> Its carpet. Over the creeds
> And masterpieces our wheels go.

Ted Hughes writes:

> He wanted to sing about her
> He didn't want comparisons with the
>   earth or anything to do with it
>
> Oversold like detergents
> He did not even want words
> Waving their long tails in public
> With their prostitutes exclamations
>
> He wanted to sing very clear.

Their poetry, struggling to break through the chinks in the dark cavern, throbs with the disturbing vibrations of modern civilization.

It is confirming to note that both poets, in their own different ways, affirm the Romantic conception of art, of poets as 'the hierophants of an unapprehended inspiration: the mirrors of the gigantic shadows which futurity casts upon the·present . . .'[10] In an interview about his work, Ted Hughes claimed that, at the present moment, there is:

> a pervasive and deep feeling that civilization has now disappeared completely. If it's still there, it's still here by grace of pure inertia and chance and if the whole thing has essentially vanished one had better have one's spirit invested in something that will not vanish. And this is a shifting of your foundation to completely new Holy Ground, a new divinity, one that won't be under the rubble when the churches collapse.[11]

I wish later to question Ted Hughes' new divinity, at least, as it is manifested in *Crow,* but at the moment I am anxious only to draw attention to the ambitious, indeed sublime, conception of the poet. How different it is from the prevailing view that the poet is an ordinary man, with ordinary problems, writing about ordinary things such as mortgages, cutting the lawn, earning money and dodging work. R. S. Thomas's conception of the priest-poet is, likewise, magnificent and exhilarating to contemplate:

> My work as a poet has to deal with the presentation of imaginative truth. So that there is no conflict, there's no necessary conflict between these two things at all. As a priest I am committed to the ministry of the word and the ministry of the sacraments. Well, word is metaphor, language is sacrament, the combination is perfectly simple. In presenting the Bible to my congregation I am presenting imaginative interpretation of reality. In presenting the sacrament, administering the sacrament of bread and wine to the congregation I am again conveying, I'm using a means, a medium of contact with reality . . . But you see how these do impinge on each other and there should be no necessary conflict at all. People, no doubt, are worried by the use of the word imagination, because imagination to many people has a fictional connotation, fictional overtones. Of course, I'm using the word imagination in its Coleridgean sense, which is the highest means known to the human psyche of getting into contact

---

[10] Shelley in *A Defence of Poetry.*
[11] Ted Hughes in *The London Magazine* (January 1971).

with the ultimate reality: imaginative truth is the most immediate way of presenting ultimate reality to a human being.[12]

The comments speak eloquently for themselves. They take us out from the isolated pools and stagnant ditches and immerse us, once again, in the deep metaphysical current of English poetry.

IV

I want now to consider the development of each poet in the light cast by their latest volumes. First, I will look at R. S. Thomas, then Ted Hughes.

From the beginning, R. S. Thomas' poetry has been firmly rooted in a landscape, a religion and a community, and it has always embodied conflicting views, desires and interpretations. The conflict, for example in the early compressed portrait of Iago Prytherch, *A Peasant,*[13] was between a certain admiration for the physical solidity of the man and a certain disquiet over the spiritual emptiness of his mind. In R. S. Thomas' early work, spiritual beauty and existential fact collide with dramatic energy and fuse with startling effects. In the lines from *January*[14] describing a wounded fox:

> the crimson seeds
> Of blood burst with a mild explosion
> Soft as excrement, bold as roses

how daring and appropriate is the marriage of opposites, the binding of 'burst' with 'mild', of 'excrement' with 'roses'. A relish for contraries, ambiguities, paradoxes darts through the poetry. And, of course, R. S. Thomas couldn't have found a richer ground for his appetite than Protestant Christianity and twentieth-century Wales. From the questioning nature of his early poetry, one feels that Thomas' faith is renewed each morning in the manner of an inward argument, a tussle between belief and doubt, death and resurrection, spirit and flesh. And his vision of Wales is, in similar manner, dialectical. It is, as defined in his early poetry, a country torn between the demands of traditional culture and modern civilization, wrenched forward by the gaudy pressures of the present, pulled back by a history 'brittle with

---

[12] R. S. Thomas in *Poetry Wales* (Spring 1972).

[13] *Song at the Year's Turning* (Hart-Davis, 1955).

[14] ibid.

relics'. In his best poems, as in *A Peasant, A Welsh Landscape,
Song at the Year's Turning,*[15] *January, Invasion, On the Farm,*[16]
these opposites are yoked lyrically together in a state of high
tension.

In the later books of R. S. Thomas, however, one detects what
can only be described as . poetic exhaustion. In *Not That He
Brought Flowers,*[17] for example, many of the poems are
rhythmically impotent. Others border heavily on rational
exposition. Still others deteriorate into moralistic rants like the
following:

> Have a care;
> This wealth is for the few
> And chosen. Those who crowd
> A small window dirty it
> With their breathing, though sublime
> And inexhaustible the view.[18]

More worrying still, a number of poems seemed in danger of
parodying their original forerunners. A certain form of
expression, once agile and distinctive in movement, seemed to be
freezing into a mannerism. The poetry was becoming lifeless
because predictable. One was beginning to expect 'the gnarled
hands on the cheque book', death 'bitter as the soil' and the
blackbird's accompaniment 'that promises them love'. Too heavy
a reliance on past methods and achievements suggested that the
original insights, so boldly projected in the early poetry, were
beginning to decay into habitual responses, gestures without
substance, symbols without the flash of vision.

At the same time, in an occasional poem in the later works, one
became aware of a new energy, audaciously heading out into
deep water, an effort to fashion, what we can now see clearly after
the publication of *H'm,* another poetic style, an effort to open up
a new ocean for poetic exploration. In, for example, the poem
That all the old preoccupations are cast afresh, given new life
and a disturbing universality:

> And endlessly the days go on ·
> With their business. Lovers make their appearance
> And vanish. The germ finds its way
> From the grass to the snail to the liver to the grass.

---

[15] ibid.
[16] ibid.
[17] *Not That He Brought Flowers* (Hart-Davis, 1968).
[18] *From the Small Window,* ibid.

The shadow of the tree falls
On our acres like a crucifixion,
With a bird singing in the branches
What its shrill species has always sung,
Hammering its notes home
One by one into our brief flesh.[19]

The poem, in fact, points us directly to the best poems in *H'm*.
It has the same freedom of line, the same disturbing breadth of
vision, as can be quickly appreciated if we compare it to the
following stanzas from *Repeat:*

He touched it. It exploded.
Man was inside with his many
Devices. He turned from him as from his own
Excrement. He could not stomach his grin.

I'll mark you, he thought. He put his finger
On him. The result was poetry
The lament of Job, Aeschylus,
The grovelling of the theologians.
Man went limping through life, holding
His side.[20]

In *H'm* R. S. Thomas was seeking to create a radical mythology
for the twentieth century, a mythology dependent for its vitality
on that war between polarities which I referred to earlier, but this
time conceived within the mechanical and artificial environment
created by the Industrial Revolution. In *H'm* the opposites are
seen as transcending the particular contexts of place and
community and envisaged as universal energies, God and the
Machine, Theocracy and Technocracy, and, as the following
quotation shows, Poetry and Production:

The tins marched to the music
Of the conveyor belt. A billion
Mouths opened. Production,
Production, the wheels

Whistled. Among the forests
Of metal the one human
Sound was the lament of
The poets for deciduous language.

The vast conception of human struggle, seen as existing
embryonically since The Fall, served to resurrect the rather over-

---

[19] *Not That He Brought Flowers.*
[20] *H'm.*

worn themes of Thomas' poetry and provided, at the same time, material wholly appropriate to a free-ranging style with which in his middle period he was occasionally experimenting.

I want, finally, to register one important critical reservation about the achievement of *H'm*. I have implicitly praised the free-wheeling lines for the poetry is thus able to span disparate experiences, experiences widely separated by the divisions of space and time, and forge unexpected connections. But, often, in *H'm*, the actual words lack resonance, depth, density. *The poetry lacks physical energy*. It limps across the page. Let me give two examples:

> Mostly it was wars
> With their justifications
> Of the surrender of values
> For which they thought. Between
> Them they laid their plans
> For the next, exempted
> From compact by the machines
> Exigencies . . .[21]

> There were people around;
> I would have spoken with them.
> But the situation has got beyond
> Language. Machines were invented
> To cope, but they were also limited
> By our expectations . . .[22]

The words are without lyrical energy and poetic substance. The meanings are explicit, prosaic. The sentences are like those in a treatise or a drab political manifesto: 'But the situation has got beyond language': 'Machines were invented to cope': 'the surrender of values'. The words are void of *texture*. This is true, although to a lesser extent, even in the poems which until this point I have implicitly admired. If R. S. Thomas' new poems are more ambitious than his earlier ones, they, yet, lack the verbal music of his first volumes. This is a major loss. And yet, in the same breath, one wishes to point to the positive intention of *H'm*, the effort to break into new ground, to widen the scope of contemporary poetry, to bring a new burden of universality to poetic themes. R. S. Thomas has opened the door to a new poetry. It must be hoped that younger poets may now step through.

[21] From *Digest*.
[22] From *Remedies*.

V

Ted Hughes' first volume of poetry *The Hawk in the Rain*[23] was
published in 1957. The book offered the reader a disparate and
uneven collection of poems. Some of the poems were heavy with
rhetoric and near-clichés, others were surprisingly delicate and
beautifully precise. Some of the poems strutted melodramatically,
others were written at a distance, were cool and analytical. And a
few of the poems stood out with a strange and almost visionary
intensity.

It was very much a *first* book. The writer was experimenting
with different forms and metres, trying to find his own particular
voice, his own particular interpretation of experience. Often the
experimentation clouds the experience. In the following lines for
example:

> But all his efforts to concoct
> The old heroic bang from their money and praise,
> From the parent's pointing fingers and the child's amaze,
> Even from the burning of his wretched bays
> Have left him wrecked . . .[24]

One can see that the metrical and rhyming structure has forced
the experience into an artificial and somewhat archaic shape.
(One wouldn't have expected to find the words 'the child's amaze'
in English poetry at any point after Wilfred Owen.) At other
moments in the volume, one is aware of rather pretentious poems,
showing stylistic polish, but no impelling content; exercises in
poetic phraseology such as:

> You had to come
> Calling my singularity
> In scorn,
> Imprisonment.
>
> It contained content
> That, now, at liberty
> In your generous embrace,
> At once, in rich Rome,
> Caractacus,
> I mourn.[25]

In a different vein are the diffuse, moralizing and banal poems,
such as *The Hag* and *Law in the Country*. Elsewhere one senses

---

[23] Ted Hughes, *The Hawk in the Rain* (Faber & Faber).
[24] From *The Famous Poet*.
[25] From *Two Phases*.

in the poetry the genuine struggle of the poet anxious to create a
true form for his own unique responses. In the opening stanza of
the title poem, the dense accumulation of alliterative words points
to a powerful experience desperately seeking order and
permanence:

> I drown in the drumming ploughland, I drag up
> Heel after heel from the swallowing of the earth's mouth,
> From clay that clutches my each step to the ankle
> With the habit of the dogged grave, but the hawk
> Effortlessly at height hangs his still eye.

The power of the experience is generally felt in these lines but
somehow not actually embodied. The words clog their meanings.
The rhythms are contorted and turn in on themselves. It has an
unmistakable poetic quality, but it is not achieved poetry.

Three poems stand out, it seems to me, in *The Hawk in the
Rain: Wind, The Thought-Fox,* and *The Horses.* They are too
well known to need quotation. It is significant, though, that the
three poems are all concerned with Nature, with imposing
animals and fierce elements. They are also all written in free verse
held tightly together by alliterative tensions and sharply perceived
imagery. These poems held out a promise of a poetry with muscle
and sinew, rich with unclouded perceptions and a primitive
sympathy for natural energies. The promise was largely fulfilled
by the two following volumes, *Lupercal* and *Wodwo.*

The most successful poems in these volumes were, once again,
preoccupied with the alert world of the wild animal: the pike, the
thrush, the otter and the hawk. It was as if the physical vitality of
nature, unchecked by the doubts and burdens of self-
consciousness, was being admired for its instinctive poise and
unquestioning right to life and action:

> . . . Mozart's brain had it, and the shark's mouth
> That hungers down the blood-smell even to a leak of
> 							its own
> Side and devouring of itself: efficiency which
> Strikes too streamlined for any doubt to pluck at it
> Or obstruction deflect.
>
> With a man it is otherwise . . .[26]

With a man it is otherwise because of the power, as we saw in the
first chapter, to symbolize, to stand outside of the timeless flux of

---

[26] From the poem *Thrushes, Lupercal* (Faber & Faber).

nature by saying verbs with a past tense and a future as well as a present. The power to symbolize isolates man from nature and renders his own being problematic to himself. The division, then, between man and nature, in Ted Hughes' work, would seem to be sound enough. But Coleridge's suggestion *that man sees in nature those qualities he himself places there,* casts another light on poems like *Hawk* and *Pike*. Are they descriptive nature poems? Or are they poems which select certain animals to symbolize and celebrate *the particular qualities* of violence and manic action? Are the animals more like emblems in a developing mythology than portraits of actual beasts? These questions have disturbing implications. If we decide the poems are descriptive, we can admire their verbal qualities, but, ultimately, must point to their limited range — for what can they tell us about the delights and burdens of human experience? If we decide the poems are essentially symbolic, evoking the nature of our experience, then we must point to their brutality, their failure to recognize the human powers of creativity, tenderness, love and transcendence. The publication of *Crow* suggests we should adopt the latter interpretation.

Before discussing the content of *Crow* I would like, briefly, to refer again to its style. I have mentioned already its liturgical quality. Lines, like the concluding stanza from *Littleblood:*

O littleblood, drumming in a cow's skull
Dancing with a gnat's feet
With an elephant's nose with a crocodile's tail.

Grown so wise grown so terrible
Sucking death's mouldy tits.

Sit on my finger, sing in my ear, O littleblood.

do have that verbal texture and energy which I found wanting in *H'm*. The lines drive their extraordinary imagery into the marrow of one's bones. It is part of Ted Hughes' genius to be able to convey immense clustering sensations through taut rhythms and original images. Although in *Crow*, it must be admitted that many of the poems lack economy. There is an excess of shocking imagery ('Horrors — hairy and slobbery, glossy and raw': 'He split his Mammy like a melon/He was drenched with gore'). And sensational words ('sod', 'bollocks', 'bastard', 'jackboots', 'blood-spittle', 'guts', etc. etc.) are employed too frequently to gain their questionable effects. The work suffers from a crudity, a pounding brutality of language. The poems scream into our brains and, in so doing, destroy the necessary and defining limits of art. In a very short time, as is invariably the case with sensational matter, we cease to respond. *We are unable to respond.* The verbal sensationalism that disfigures many of the poems in *Crow* registers, I believe, a deeper failure, a failure in interpretation, which, as it returns us to our questions about the intention of Ted Hughes' earlier animal poetry, I now wish to discuss.

If there is doubt about whether *Hawk* refers to energies and actions beyond the particular species, there can be no doubt about Crow. Crow symbolizes the indestructible will to survive. He symbolizes energy, endurance, the will to power. *Examination at the Womb-door* ends with Crow being even more powerful than Death:

Who is stronger than hope? *Death.*
Who is stronger than the will? *Death.*
Stronger than love? *Death.*
Stronger than life? *Death.*

But who is stronger than death? *Me evidently*
Pass, Crow.

But we need to ask *how* does Crow survive, in *what sort of world* does he survive, and what does he survive *for*? It is in answering these questions that we confront the failure of *Crow* for, in truth, the book projects a nightmare universe stripped of meaning and worth. In *Lineage* we are given the black theology of Crow:

In the beginning was Scream
Who begat Blood . . .
Who begat God
Who begat Nothing
Who begat Never
Never Never Never

Who begat Crow

Screaming for Blood
Grubs, crusts
Anything

Trembling featherless elbows in the nest's filth.

Throughout the volume, creation is seen as a disease, 'the virus of God', a dark jest in which we are unwittingly embroiled, a jest which only Crow, through a series of evasions and cunning strategies, is able to turn to his own advantage. The book thus represents a total inversion of human values. Birth is seen as 'A Kill', perception as blindness, everything as being grounded in nothing:

> So finally there was nothing.
> It was put inside nothing.
> Nothing was added to it.
> And to prove it didn't exist
> Squashed flat as nothing with nothing.[27]

In such an absurd world, a world shot through with pointlessness, the only aspiration left is the one to survive *at all costs*.

In the interview, which I have already quoted, Ted Hughes talked about —

> a complete abolition of everything that's been up to this point and Crow is what manages to drag himself out of it in fairly good morale.

But, in as much as *Crow* is celebrating *the mere act of survival and making it appear the only possible value,* we must object that the book denying the powers of love, creativity and reparation is profoundly nihilistic. Ian Robinson and David Sims define this objection extremely well:

> But Crow, as that which can survive, the central symbol of the work, is the thing centrally wrong. For Crow (unlike Hamlet) insists that survival is in itself the criterion of value. But one may well ask whether Crow is fit to live, or whether it matters much whether he survives or not, if he survives hope, love, life and death.[28]

It was Darwin who, in the nineteenth century, made current the notion of 'the survival of the fittest'. Transferred from nature (where it may or may not be wholly applicable) to society it becomes a reductive creed—for on such terms a gangster or a thug become more worthy than the prophet, the poet, the seminal philosopher and the idealist. Such a transference is also philosophically false for it is blind to that dimension of human existence opened by the power to symbolize: that dimension in which is to be found all those subjective achievements in morality, culture and religion, distinguishing man from nature. The failure of *Crow* consists in its inability to find the essence of man. Not only doesn't *Crow* find that Holy Ground, that new

---

[27] From *Conjuring in Heaven*.
[28] In *The Human World*, No. 9, November 1972.

divinity,[29] which Ted Hughes believes we must discover before the threatening darkness falls, it also, by its savage assault on human kind, makes it even more difficult to discover and symbolize.

VI

It is always difficult to express clearly a judgement about a poet's achievement. I have looked at R. S. Thomas and Ted Hughes because they are important contemporary writers who have had the audacity to throw open the doors and windows of a stuffy house. They have made possible a new poetry, broad, free-ranging, essentially mythopoeic. That is a considerable achievement. However, it is important, also, to be aware of the weaknesses that attend new movements so that those who follow may be able to rectify them and so find the vital balance of art. The weakness, I have suggested, in *H'm,* is that the language is not generally strong enough to carry its bold cargoes. The failure of *Crow,* I have argued, is that it is propounding a view of life which deprives man of any purpose and, in the midst of suffering and confusion, of any powers of reparation. It offers us only a black rainbow arched over an abyss where fly violent and unselfconscious creatures. Such a bleak and desperate vision denies us the hope of poetry, conceived as a humanizing and liberating force.

I have also argued that while it is important for literary criticism not to expend too much energy on what is ephemeral, it is yet essential for it to seek out the best of what is being currently published and be ready here not merely to praise but to scrupulously compare and evaluate. In taking two contemporary poets and in delineating their progression towards a mythopoeic form of poetry, I hope to have provided one example of the style of alert criticism we should be encouraging in our students. Such critical work, however, though it will generally take place in the English Department, must not be isolated from the intellectual life of the College, an intellectual life which should be characterized by a widespread preoccupation with seminal ideas, generative principles and political possibilities. Each Depart-mental activity, every discerning act of criticism, should be seen to visibly add to the whole intellectual ferment of the College. It is to this *need* for a greater involvement in living ideas—

---

[29] I would like to point out that Ted Hughes' *The Iron Man* does succeed here where

I italicize the word 'need' because no-one can pretend it yet exists — that I would like now to turn my attention.[30]

---

[30] For another critical study of *Crow* see David Holbrook's *Ted Hughes' Crow and the Longing for Non-Being* in *The Black Rainbow*, (Heinemann Educational Books).

SIX

An Existential Approach to

Colleges of Education

By an act that is both creative and unconscious—for it is not 'I' who actualise the possible, but 'it' actualises itself through me—the bridge of symbol is thrown between the living 'here' and 'there'. Suddenly, necessarily and completely the world comes into being out of the totality of received and remembered elements: and as it is an individual who apprehends the world, there is for each individual a singular world.

Oswald Spengler

I

*The Need for Philosophical and
Educational Premises*

Colleges of Education are now facing a crisis of meaning. It is a crisis that demands generous energies, a new influx of philosophical ideas and a willingness to explore modes of teaching radically different from those traditionally found in establishments of higher education. It is a crisis that, above all, demands fundamental discussion as to the true ideals of education in a rapidly emerging technocratic society. If the crisis is not properly recognized, and if false bureaucratic and mechanical answers are allowed to smother it (as they will attempt to) then a chance for renewal and transformation will have been lost with the result that an influential sector of the educational system may be oppressed for decades to come.

In order to stress the common nature of the problems facing the colleges, I would like to begin by quoting a summary describing the findings of a survey conducted by the National Union of Students:

The National Union of Students conducted a national survey at the end of 1969 in which answers were obtained from 46 colleges and over 11,000 students. Of the total, 61% of the men and 54.1% of the women did not believe that their course would adequately equip them for teaching. In particular over 56% of the total thought there should be more time spent on teaching practice, almost three-quarters thought that the lack of emphasis on professional development was the most serious deficiency in their course, and 87% felt their college lecturers should be more in touch with classroom realities.

This picture can be filled out in more detail with the aid of other local surveys. Leicester education students, for example, tested opinion before submitting recommendations to their area training organisation. One of the most startling findings, after polling St Paul's College, the Domestic Science College, and the City of Leicester College, was that there was a favourable response, ranging from 61% in St Paul's to 83% at the City of Leicester, for the idea that students should spend a complete year's teaching before the third year of their course.

Overwhelming majorities at these three colleges felt that the need for compensatory education, particularly in educational priority areas, was not covered adequately, rather smaller majorities felt that they were not being sufficiently prepared for teaching in teams and across subject boundaries. In general, 63% of the Leicester students felt that their education course work was unsatisfactory—73% considered the history of education to be of little value—whereas large majorities thought it essential to be trained in improvising with inadequate equipment, in teaching mixed ability classes, and in relating to parents and social and psychiatric services.[1]

The criticisms embodied in this account constitute a challenge. But what should be the response of the colleges? An argument based on number is not of itself a sufficient reason for re-organizing the over-all framework of a college, for next year (or the year after) the numbers may change. Clearly, thorough thinking must transcend numerical wishes and the general tyranny of numbers—and yet the criticisms must be heeded. What can be done? Can the criticisms thrown up from the student body be placed and partially justified in a wider context of a philosophy of education? If this were possible, it would mean that the colleges could change—*not* as is the obsession of our times, for the sake of change—nor at the dictates of percentages, but *because a coherent philosophy made radical good-sense of such and such changes, and not others*. Here, then, we arrive at our central problem. What should be our common purpose in education? And what implications does it entail for our practice

[1] Quoted from *Fit to Teach* edited by Bruce Kemble (Hutchinson Educational).

and organization in Colleges of Education? These questions must be answered if the present crisis (indicated only vaguely by the figures I have quoted) in the training of teachers is to be truly met and overcome.

I would like to begin to consider an answer to 'what should be our over-all philosophy?' by looking first of all at the educational background of the majority of students who enter a College of Education. Before coming to the college, the students have been studying for two, three or four years academic courses: five to eight 'O' levels: two to three 'A' levels. In these studies they have done reasonably well, but not brilliantly. Under the pressure of study it is to be assumed that most of them have absorbed the notion that learning consists of *receiving, recording, memorizing and returning the right information.* At the same time they have become accustomed to conceive of education as conveniently dividing into self-contained units of knowledge: French, Maths, English, Chemistry, RI and so on. Furthermore they will have come to regard the more personal powers of being: the powers of being, the powers of imagining, creating, evaluating and improvising as having little or no place inside the educational process.

We must remember that when it comes to mass examination preparation, most schools have not changed much since Dickens wrote *Hard Times.*

The notion of education described or possibly parodied (but only slightly) by Dickens in his polemical novel has a long history behind it and is rooted, as we are now beginning to see, in a false mechanical conception of knowledge which originated with the seventeenth-century philosophies of reason.[2] In the last ten years we find in the first stages of our educational system a steady moving away from the idea of learning as the burden of formal and endless memorizing. Indeed, it is fascinating to see that the *Primary School Report* published *as early as 1931* had this to say:

> The principle which is here described will be challenged by no one who has grasped the idea that life is a process of growth in which there are successive changes, each with its own specific character and needs . . .
>
> (The curriculum) appeals less to passive obedience and more to the sympathy, social spirit and imagination of the children, relies less on mass instruction, and more on the encouragement of individual and

[2] For an analysis of the world-picture based on reason see my *Mechanical-World-Picture* in *The Black Rainbow* (Heinemann Educational Books, 1975).

group work, and treats the school in short, not as the antithesis of life, but as its complement and commentary.

Such a living conception of education has been confirmed and extended in our own times by the *Plowden Report, The Middle Years of Schooling Working Paper No. 22* and the *Newsom Report* and, as a result, we find in our primary and middle schools (where, be it noted, with the general lifting of the terrors and securities of the 11+, examination and mass-assessment have retreated)—a growing emphasis on the powers of the imagination and the needs of the child *as a whole being*. And yet, without doubt, students who in three years will be teaching in those very schools, enter Colleges of Education with very different, mechanical and Gradgrind assumptions. In this dichotomy, we can begin to detect what should be the prime responsibility of our Colleges of Education.

It should be the function of the College of Education to present both in the content of its professional courses and in its own style of teaching a radically different concept of education from that which the students have come to accept as normal. This is where a College of Education should be essentially different from a university. The university (though this is changing in some places) continues to build on the foundations laid down by the 'A' level methods of study—it tends to narrow the students' interests even further and demands that he acquire greater knowledge of his particular subject. The university creates the specialist, the man proficient in one area of knowledge, but generally deficient elsewhere. A College of Education has, I am suggesting, a radically different path to follow. Unlike the university, it must begin to broaden out the students' curiosities, it must attempt to reveal the essential connections between forms of knowledge and forms of artistic creation: it must begin to nurture and develop those powers of feeling and imagining, of improvising and creating, which have been dulled and half-lost under the relentless demands of sixth-form academic studies. In a College of Education, the stress should therefore be on the personal, experimental, collaborative nature of knowing and creating. Only in this way can the student begin to discover and develop those broad sympathies and interests which he will need constantly to draw on if he is to teach creatively in the classroom.

I would like here to give one brief example of the style of activity I have in mind. At Aberystwyth I took a small group of students for one year with the purpose of encouraging them

to explore the impact of their education on their identities.
The work took the form of a long piece of written auto-
bigoraphy—which, week after week, was read by each individual and discussed. Here nothing was given that was not
recreated and presented by the individual students: their
experience (and the collaborative evaluation of that experience)
was the single sustaining centre of the work.[3]

The following quotations from one of the autobiographies
reveal the passionate, vivid, uncertain, dramatic nature of the
activity:

> I don't expect this to be easy. I shall need to add to it continuously
> and hope that it represents something reasonable by the time it is
> finished.
>
> The beginning must be most difficult of all to write—groping in
> the dark—later, when other people have talked and I have something
> to compare myself with, I might be able to rationalize. (I'm rewriting
> this now (1/12/71) because of illegibility and to make it more
> comprehensive and more comprehensible. Am amused at how
> doubtful I was to begin with). I have very little confidence at the
> moment that I'll be able to express myself at all, mostly because I have
> never done so before in any logical form. And I'm sure to be
> appallingly ashamed of the thing when its done—most because I
> don't think I work very logically—I understand but can't relate. But
> perhaps the whole process of writing it down may help to see it all as
> an entity by the time it is finished . . .
>
> I find, in spite of never having talked to this intensity in a group
> situation that I can follow people's flow, trains of thought. Am
> delighted, in Leeds I was thick academically, and I had always to feel
> inferior, quite irrationally. Now I go away exhilarated every time,
> even if it has seemed an unresponsive afternoon. I am always
> reworking, always thinking, none of it is ever futile. I learn an
> immense amount just from the talking-listening process. Makes me
> happy, gives a meaning to the rest of the course . . .
>
> We are a stillness in that room, with the movement happening
> inside and outside. Silences only a little oppressive, sometimes they
> are not at all oppressive. This is good . . . There is a shape to the
> whole thing. In patterns of weeks.

I am concerned here only to point to the degree of involvement
both individual and collaborative and to the way in which feeling
and thinking are seen racing together, both essential to the
process of discovery. *This* I am arguing, is the complex order of

---

[3] For a full study of the place of autobiography in Education see Chapter 7.

knowing/exploring/sensing that we should be concerned to promote.

I would now like to give these very qualities a philosophical basis. It would seem that for nearly 400 years, since the rise of modern science, there has been a strong intellectual movement to divorce knowledge from being, the thought from the thinker, the object from the subject. It began with the notion perpetrated by Galileo, Descartes and Kepler that we could only know what we could measure.

It was Kepler who wrote:

> The mind has been formed to understand not all sorts of things, but quantities . . . the further a thing recedes from quantities the more darkness and error inheres in it.

Kepler's dogmatic assertion was not a solitary event. It belonged to that busy movement of the Renaissance away from the palpable and infolded nature of experience towards abstraction and mechanism. The process towards an increasing abstraction can be detected not only in the philosophical formulations, in Galileo's distinction between Primary and Secondary qualities, in Descartes' definition of the body as 'a machine made by God', but also in, for example, the Protestant rebellion (destroying symbolism and ritual), in the ending of bartering and the instituting of a general currency, in the inventing of the clock and other measuring machines, and the movement, slow but certain, towards numerical democracy. Thus, life came to be interpreted through the categories of measurement, efficiency, productivity, and quantitative progress. Other modes of understanding, creating and relating, based on aesthetics, on tradition, on imagination, on morality, were quietly but determinedly discarded.

Descartes from his meditation on the nature of wax concluded:

> It is now manifest to me that bodies themselves are not properly perceived by the senses, nor by the faculty of imagination, but by the intellect alone.

The universe could only be comprehended through the forms of mathematics: both the senses with their fluctuating testimonies and the imagination with its 'blundering constructions' deceived. Poets, 'whose minds', according to Descartes, 'are stored with the most agreeable fancies' might entertain but they were utterly unequipped to tackle the primary questions of meaning and purpose. The arts might decorate society but they were void

of intellectual and social substance. And so, during the
Renaissance, a crucial dissociation between intellect and
imagination, between abstraction and sensuous perception,
between knowledge and sensibility, developed in Western man,
leading in the nineteenth century to Bentham's 'All poetry is
superstition' and Gradgrind's 'Facts, nothing but Facts' — and has
come through in our own age to a cult concerning the 'expert'
with his 'objectivity' and clinical neutrality. As I have indicated, I
believe it is this misguided obsession for pure objectivity that
underlies much of the dull and drab teaching in the higher aeons
of education.

Why is it false? It is false because it distorts the actual nature of
intellectual and creative experience. There can be no thought
outside of a person thinking, and indeed, no thinking that is not
lit up with feeling and expectation. Put another way, it could be
said that knowledge is never wholly given, it is always partly
created by the person, and always moving towards a further
possible configuration of sense and meaning. The scientist and
philosopher, Polanyi, calls all knowledge tacit; in his book *The
Tacit Dimension* he shows that knowledge must always be
experiential in nature and always groping forward:

> It appears, then, that to know that a statement is true is to know
> more than we can tell and that hence, when a discovery solves a
> problem, it is itself fraught with further intimations of an
> indeterminate range, and that furthermore, when we accept the
> discovery as true, we commit ourselves to a belief in all these as yet
> undisclosed, perhaps as yet unthinkable consequences.

Knowledge is part of a living enduring process which can only
take place *inside the person.* There is thus, always, at source, a
rich and inevitable relationship between concept and biography,
philosophy and existence. During the last few decades many
psycho-analytical concepts have entered our language and
become commonplace expressions: archetype, ego, repression,
introvert, extrovert, regression. We tend, indeed, to use these
words almost unthinkingly as if they pointed to events and
processes which have always been seen as an essential part of
human experience. We forget that the words carry a heavy cargo
of interpretations and that these interpretations were forged by
the peculiarly powerful and frequently disturbing efforts made by
gifted and courageous individuals seeking to comprehend their
own identities. Here is how Jung in *Memories, Dreams,
Reflections* relates his theories to his own life:

The knowledge I was concerned with, or was seeking, still could not be found in the science of those days. I myself had to undergo the original experience, and, moreover, try to plant the results of my experience in the soil of reality; otherwise they would have remained subjective assumptions . . .

Today I can say that I have never lost touch with my initial experiences. All my works, all my creative activity, has come from those initial fantasies and dreams which began in 1912, almost fifty years ago. Everything that I accomplished in later life was already contained in them, although at first only in the form of emotions and images.

My science was the only way I had of extricating myself from that chaos . . .

The years when I was pursuing my inner images were the most important in my life — in them everything essential was decided. It all began then: the later details are only supplements and clarifications of the material that burst forth from the unconscious and at first swamped me. It was the *prima materia* for a lifetime's work.

Freud's theories, like Jung's, were also deeply rooted in inward obsession and disturbance. *The Interpretation of Dreams,* proclaiming dreams to be the royal road to the unconscious, had its origins in Freud's self-analysis generated by the feelings of anxiety and depression which overwhelmed him after his father's death in 1896.[4] Many problems are raised by the essential biographical element in human knowledge: problems concerning subjectivity and objectivity, personality and universality. Here, however, I am only anxious to draw attention to the dense intertwining of theory and existence. It may be objected that this is true only in the humanities and not in the more impersonal fields of scientific enquiry. But, even here, I would argue, there remains in the very·process of complex symbolization a vital and irreducible element of human interpretation and creation. The biologist J. Z. Young has written:

In some sense we literally create the world we speak about. Therefore our physical science is not simply a set of reports about an outside world. It is also a report about ourselves and our relations to that world, whatever the latter may be like.[5]

Science, for all its utility and apparent objectivity, still cannot be fully comprehended without reference to its source in the human mind. The intricate schemata of each science forms, in the first

[4] See Charles Rycroft in *New York Review*, 10 August 1972.
[5] Quoted by Bill Allchin in *Tract 9, The Archetypal Context of Political Experience.*

place, an imposing artefact of the analytical intelligence.

Given this understanding of the symbolizing activity of the psyche, the dangers of a fanatical objectivity[6] become only too obvious. Again I would like to quote Polanyi here:

> The declared aim of modern science is to establish a strictly detached, objective knowledge. Any falling short of this ideal is accepted only as a temporary imperfection, which we must aim at eliminating. But suppose that tacit thought forms an indispensable part of all knowledge, then the ideal of eliminating all personal elements of knowledge would, in effect, aim at the destruction of all knowledge. The ideal of exact science would turn out to be fundamentally misleading and possibly a source of devastating fallacies.

If Polanyi's thinking is right, and it is confirmed by many other studies[7] as well as forming one of the philosophical premises on which many primary schools are now run, the implications for Colleges of Education must be clear. I think, perhaps the most positive way of seeing Polanyi's remarks is to remind ourselves of the connection between enthusiasm and discovery, between delight and education. Henry Mayhew in his *London Labour and the London Poor* expresses the essential relationship between feeling and thinking I am here anxious to stress.

> We do not remember how our own tastes have been formed, nor do we in our zeal stay to reflect how the tastes of a people generally are created: and, consequently we cannot perceive that a habit of enjoying any matter whatsoever can only be induced in the mind by linking it with some aesthetic affections.
> *The heart is the mainspring of the intellect,* and the feelings the real educers and educators of the thought.

> *Feeling must run with thinking—and thinking with feeling—or the enterprise will be barren.*
> *True knowledge is inward, tacit, experiential: never merely a body of inert facts.*

Here, I suggest, lies a sane structure on which to build a radically new education for the colleges. Such an education is, in

---

[6] Consider, for example, the belief in objectivity revealed by the following: 'Most sociologists, psychiatrists, educationalists and psychologists are largely innumerate, to use Lord Snow's term: they tend to think in verbal terms only, and fail to criticize the model on the *only grounds* which are really relevant to its correctness, that is quantitative ones', H. Eysenck, *The Inequality of Man*, (Temple Smith) (My italics).

[7] See, for example, Lewis Mumford's *The Pentagon of Power* (Secker & Warburg) Roger Poole's *Towards Deep Subjectivity* (Allen Lane/The Penguin Press) and Werner Pelz's *The Scope of Understanding in Sociology* (Routledge & Kegan Paul).

fact, being slowly explored with many risks and with inevitable failings, in our primary and middle schools. It is also, of course, the concept of education which informs such indispensable books as Sybil Marshall's *An Experiment in Education,* Herbert Kohl's *36 Children* and David Holbrook's *English for the Rejected.* To develop the practice of the colleges on such principles would be to anchor them securely in the intertwining realities of sound educational philosophy and the growing practice of our schools. I wish now to consider the practical implications of such a commitment to 'tacit knowing'.

II

Present Failings: Future Possibilities

I have argued that students coming into Colleges of Education bring with them an assumption that education consists of learning all the relevant facts which conveniently congregate under the various subject labels. I also suspect that, particularly among those interested in teaching very young children, the students' intuitions, intuitions, that is, about children's real needs as they are expressed in their play, phantasy and relationships, conflict with this interiorized conception of mechanical learning. Unfortunately, there is a danger that their conception of education — which I have endeavoured to show is false — is further confirmed by the practices of the college and that the students' wiser intuitions (in need of discipline and clarification) wither through neglect.

Let me give one simple example of where this often happens. I understand that for a number of years now, students, in a number of colleges, on their very first encounter with schools, during their first observation period, are asked to concentrate their energies on administering an objective reading-test. Such a request with its emphasis on isolating the child, on establishing impersonal 'clinical' conditions, in order that certain statistical generalities can be arrived at, can only bolster the already strong technical notion of education as measurement and, at the same time, undermine those vital, but more elusive intuitions about the nature of children. I am not against these tests as such: they may well have a limited purpose in the study of reading problems but I am suggesting that on the student's *first visit to school* total attention should be given to the over-all experience of the school. Students should be urged to see the children *as children* (not abstractions plotted on a white sheet of paper) responding and developing, or otherwise, in the community of the classroom. This is not as easy as it sounds: and students would probably gain from being asked to read such books as Kohl's *36 Children* or Edward Blishen's *Roaring Boys* before actually starting on their period of observation.

More generally, there is a danger that the teaching in the colleges will continue on the same lines as sixth-form academic studies with all the attendant limitations. Certainly many students in the colleges strike me as being overwhelmed by the relentless demands for notes, files, essays, coming from many different, unrelated departments. The very amount of work asked from them militates against the more creative and personal education I am arguing for.

I want, later, to make a plea for more collaboration between Departments for it is only by a drawing together of imaginative and intellectual disciplines that any unity can be organically created and a genuine education begin. Here, however, I want to continue by developing my remarks on the academic nature of many studies within the colleges.

Morrison and McIntyre in *Teachers & Teaching* make this observation on the study of psychology in their book:

> One may first note that the aspects of psychology which have been stressed in college courses have tended to be the same as those predominating in general courses on the psychology of human behaviour in Universities: perception, learning, thinking, cognitive development, individual differences. In contrast social and clinical psychology have been relatively neglected . . . The aim has been to see that students should acquire a *knowledge* of psychology.

The problem is that the colleges seem to be following in the tracks set by the universities rather than seeking out a richer and more relevant pattern of studies for themselves. The desire to cover a field *analytically* to begin with theory and abstract formulation (which the first-year students seem to find extremely difficult to understand) can be seen to stem from the tendency in the Colleges of Education to imitate the universities. It is thought that the university gives an imprint of respectability *to certain forms of enquiry and not to others*. Such an attitude is stultifying because it destroys with one swift blow intellectual diversity and the right of all educational enterprises to improvise and experiment.

Noam Chomsky has defended the academic study of the social
sciences in the following way:

> The social and behavioural studies should be seriously studied not
> only for their intrinsic merit, but so that the student can be made
> quite aware of exactly how little they have to say about the problems
> of man and society that really matter.

This constitutes a defense for the social sciences academically
conceived: I think there is another approach open to social
studies both more imaginative in method and more ambitious in
scope, which it would be wholly appropriate for Colleges of
Education to pioneer. This approach has been called
phenomenological: it begins by considering actual experience
and moves outwards to certain conclusions which may or may not
be generally true. The philosopher John Macquarrie describes
the phenomenological approach in this way:

> The point about phenomenology is that it offers a description in
> depth, so to speak, causing us to notice features that we ordinarily fail
> to notice, removing hindrances that stand in the way of our seeing,
> exhibiting the essential rather than the accidental, showing
> interrelation, that may lead to a quite different view from the one that
> we get when the phenomena is considered in isolation.[8]

In the course of phenomenological enquiry, layers of meaning
are unfolded, different interpretations revealed, and slowly a
complex, composite picture of whoever or whatever is being
studied (it may be an individual child, a class of children, a
school, a family, a factory, an office, a small community) is built
up.

A fine example of the sort of phenomenological analysis I am
suggesting as a method of study for Colleges of Education is R. D.
Laing and A. Esterson's *Families of Schizophrenics* which has
been described as follows:

> Rather than treating a case of schizophrenia as *one* thing possessed
> by *one* person and regarded as his or her unique problem, Laing and
> Esterson tape-recorded interviews with the families of schizophrenics,
> such that the versions, points of view, perspectives, of the family can
> be compared with each other and with the point of view or
> perspective of the patient himself. The results are startling,
> electrifying. Suddenly, by an astute collocation and comparison of
> the perspectives of the family and of the patient (which are always in

[8] John Macquarrie, *Existentialism* (Penguin).

flagrant contradiction) the actual reasons why this 'patient' became mentally unstable are revealed.[9]

Such analysis is in the mode of the sensitive documentary which explores a reality by honestly and fastidiously structuring the many and various evaluations and meanings which people bring to illuminate the particular subject or area being investigated. It is, for example, the method employed by Charles Parker and Ewan McColl in their Radio Ballads. In an important article on the Radio Ballads Charles Parker quoted first Goethe and then Eisenstein as follows:

> In nature we never see anything isolated, but everything in connection with something else which is before it, beside it, under it and over it.
>
> GOETHE

> Montage is an idea that arises from the collision of independent shots — shots even opposite to one another.
>
> EISENSTEIN

And then commented:

> We are really talking about Montage, and what such a sequence demands of the listener, therefore, is that his stance be one of anticipating collision, not fusion, as the source of continuity. Not a narrator interpreting the evidence and handing down a smoothly blended conclusion, but the listener providing, as it were, his own narration, as he himself resolves the intellectual challenge of the successive collisions. The listener is really engaging in an unspoken dialogue with the work, and with the producer/author behind the work; his conclusions emerge at first hand, as experience which is unique to him but which also partakes of the universally available experience held in the sequence.[10]

The dynamic form of the Radio Ballad, offering a montage of varied judgements, assumptions and perspectives, is determined, then, by a sensitive understanding of the multifarious nature of human society and demands from the listener a similarly sensitive and poised response.

How could such an approach be developed inside the educational studies of a College of Education? The possibilities are enormous: and if they were to be fully realized they would

---

[9] Roger Poole in *Towards Deep Subjectivity* (Allen Lane/Penguin Press).

[10] *Views. The Listener*, 25 January, 1973. Later in the same article Charles Parker attacked the 'literal, expository documentary style which deals with things in a straightforward way' and which so easily become 'a snare and a delusion'.

need to draw on many skills from many departments. Let me suggest here a few such possibilities.

1. In the first term of the first year the close study of the students' own experience of school can be made. It could be conducted in the manner of the work in autobiography which I have already mentioned and which I will describe at length in the next chapter. The different individual responses to various teachers, types of school, subject-matter as revealed in the various autobiographies could be compared and, through a delicate process of collaboration initiated by the tutor, evaluated. Recent ideas about social class, about language codes, about play, competition, learning, symbolism, could be slowly introduced and discussed where they clarify the particular experience in question.

2. Various studies with small groups could be made of the mass media, including studies of newspapers, comics, pop music, magazines, television, 'news', advertising. Again, the work would begin by giving form to the particular responses of specific groups of people. Here different groups could be taken: children, adolescents, families, working people, students, etc., and, through collaboration, a complete picture of the reality etched. As the picture takes form, various commentaries like Raymond Williams' *Communications* and Fred Inglis' *The Imagery of Power* and Vance Packard's *The Hidden Persuaders* could be presented so that possibilities for the evaluation of the emerging experience are constantly opening out. Such work could sometimes take the form of written reports and at other times the form of the documentary. Here, as Charles Parker has pointed out, it is essential that the student be introduced to the skills of recording voices:

> A tape-recorder should be seen to be as indispensable to the teacher in training and in practice as a typewriter or fountain pen. Skill in handling microphones and acoustic environment and technical mixing of sound sources etc should be axiomatic. The tools must be there, and in plenty! Or frustration will turn the student against all he could and should be doing.[11]

The need for skill and materials in the field again serves to point to the essential collaborative nature of phenomenological study.

3. Another study could examine the different responses children show towards their schools. A study of this nature would

---

[11] Charles Parker in *Tract 3: Towards a People's Culture.*

be most fruitful if all types of school were to be included: primary, secondary, modern, grammar, comprehensive, private, public. Work might begin with the students considering and comparing their own memories and then move out to look at various children's reactions to the particular school they attend. The teaching practice in the second year might be an excellent time for this investigation. In the course of the project, notions of language and social class could be, where relevant, subtly and meaningfully introduced and questioned.

4. Reading failure in individual children could be explored in a similar way. Here the attempt would be to place the failure in the whole context of the child's experience.

While I contend that such work would be intrinsically valuable and while it also embodies a different mode of study to that of universities, it would also be worthwhile for two further reasons. First of all, it would help to connect the college to the surrounding indigenous community. It would bring students into an active and purposeful relationship with society. Furthermore, some of the work I have suggested would introduce the student to the probation officer, the child psychiatrist, the child welfare officer, the marriage guidance worker and so on. This would both help the student to understand the complexity of social work and also fulfil the demands that I quoted earlier: 'Large majorities thought it essential to be trained in . . . relating to parents and social psychiatric services'.

Secondly, it encourages students to actually listen to and recognize forms of speech different to their own. Again, this cannot be over-emphasized. Seven out of ten teachers are middle-class and seven out of ten children are working-class. It is vital that the teacher, from whatever background he may come, is able to sympathize with the particular mode of speech his children use when speaking most spontaneously. One primary school teacher in *Fit to Teach* urges '. . . it is essential that there should be more teachers who can talk to a child with a disturbed background from an emotionally sympathetic standpoint'. The activities I have been suggesting would, without doubt, develop just such a sympathy.

With such work, which is completely in accord with Polanyi's definition of the tacit and personal dimension of knowledge, I believe the Colleges of Education could begin to meet the crisis of meaning they now face. To be effective such work would have to be collaborative, and here, I contend the colleges must be less guarded and more adventurous.

I would like, finally, to suggest the following developments in English studies, where there is still a marked tendency in many colleges to weakly imitate a university course in English Literature.

1. Much more attention and time should be given to creative work: the writing of poems, stories (for children, for 'backward readers', for adolescents), plays, songs, documentaries (along the lines, perhaps, of the Radio Ballads already mentioned). There is no reason why the approach to the writing of poetry outlined in Part II should not be applied, with certain modifications, in the English departments of the colleges. Only creative individuals can teach in an alert and creative manner. If we fail to nurture the imaginative powers of the intending teacher, we fail to prepare him to teach responsively in the classroom. The following two poems were written by students in a seminar after quietly reflecting on a photograph of a fish used in the *First Series* of *English Broadsheets* (designed for twelve-year-olds):

> The open mouth, the writhing body
> Falls pitifully into pain.
> Angry waters reaches out for its stolen life,
> Heaves and sighs,
> In wait for the still breathing creature.
> The long, straining body turns wildly to be free.
> It shudders;
> Quivers;
> Screams a dying call.
>
> The skin relaxes as the water calms,
> Full weight hangs on the piercing line.
> Peace to the body.
> Peace to the water.
> Peace to the man?

(CHRISTINE BIERNAT, Final Copy)

> Agonising pain —
> Numbing feeling of cold claw;
> Tearing flesh from fish
> Animal from his environment.
> Line taut, line slack
> But escape impossible,
> Silent scream from gasping maw
> Furious bubbles fly from the surface,
> Then ripples, then calm.
> An unresisting carcass

Vanquished life.

(Final Copy)

In writing these poems (and others) the students had not only discovered a certain imaginative energy within themselves but had also prepared themselves, in the most obvious and tangible way, for introducing and developing such a theme in the classroom.

2. Much of the first term could be profitably given over to the writing of autobiography (see Chapter 7).

3. Considerable time should also be allowed for the careful discussion and evaluation of children's writing. After teaching practice a series of seminars could be arranged in which the actual writing of children collected by the students would form the main material for consideration. The various questions that cluster round creative work could, then, be raised. What is the child symbolizing? What are the qualities that mark imaginative composition? Should the teacher correct mistakes? Should revision be encouraged? What is the value of such writing?

4. Students should have the opportunity of working within a field of creative studies, where particular ideas, feelings and images may be defined in different forms: through music, film, printing, sculpture, dance, drama, poetry, prose. Here delicate collaboration between the English Department, the Drama, Art and Music Department is called for. In the third year, when students have become aware of the different possibilities locked within the various aesthetic disciplines, each student could be asked to develop a substantial piece of original work. To give some indication of the range of activities open to a collaborative course in creative studies I would like briefly to list the activities a group of students working in an Education Department chose in their last term[12] for their final projects:

(a)   Two students designed a series of lessons to introduce children to the expressive and functional uses of clay. The project was carried out with six children (between the ages of nine and eleven) from a local primary school in the art room of the Education Department. After the children had made and decorated a selection of shapes and containers, they visited a local pottery. Photographs of the children working with clay were later mounted accompanied with

---

[12] In the other two terms work in drama, art, writing, pottery, had been carefully guided by the Art tutor, John Morris and, to a lesser extent, myself.

guiding commentaries and shown in the local primary school.

(b) Three students made a tape of sounds. In the initial stages of work, a variety of improvised and accidental sounds were recorded. The students discovered that they could distort sound and so make it more expressive by playing it on a tape-recorder. Slowly the students edited their random collection of sounds into an aesthetically coherent sequence.

(c) Another student, working in a similar manner, but concentrating on deepening and distorting the actual notes made by certain musical instruments, recorded a movement of evocative sound.

(d) Eight students made a short film. They began by exploring the possibilities of the camera using an 8 mm film. Through collaborative discussion they decided on the narrative of their film, the actors, location sites etc. Eventually a script was written and the film shot.

(e) Another student concentrated on completing two groups of drawings, one developing from studies of the human figure, the other developing from imaginary forms.

(f) Two students made an animation film based on nursery rhymes. They began by drawing simple 'cut out' figures and by discussing the problem of how many frames were needed per second. In the process of making the film, they decided on the final visual narrative and the techniques required to convey its particular mood.

(g) Another student presented, at the end of the term, three exercise books of her own poems, some in their final shape, others still in process of being written.[13]

5. Students should also be encouraged not to rely passively on textbooks, but to seek out their own materials, fashion their own approaches, and under sensitive supervision, design their own worksheets and anthologies.

6. The various aspects of mass-culture should be studied. We live in an age in which the vast majority attend not to books but to television, mass-magazines, pop-music and sensational newspapers. These centralized 'cultural' forces should be understood and rigorously evaluated as well as insights coming

[13] In other years, projects, guided by John Morris, had included the making of a documentary on the Cardiganshire lead-miners, a play based on the *Mabinogion*, and a film based on the story of *Beowulf*.

from the study of literature and symbolism be brought to bear
upon them. A teacher working in any school must know how to
jump from a TV programme or a magazine like *Fabulous* or a
banal pop song, into the more genuinely literary world of ballads,
folk song, fairy tale, myths, as well as literature. (Here it is
imperative that much more time is given to the study of children's
fiction, children's lore and language — as recorded, for example,
by the Opies[14] — and the function of symbolism in games,
phantasy and spontaneous play.) In an age of mass-culture and
mass-propaganda, as described in chapter 4, the student must
also have a grasp of those ways in which he can encourage in
children and adolescents the powers of alert and positive
discrimination.

It is also essential that the professional courses in English
should be bound more firmly into the yearly teaching practices.
Indeed, I think we must question very closely the way in which
many students at the moment are asked to work in the schools.
Are students really given the best of possible conditions in which
to find their own style of teaching, in which to experiment, in
which to discover their own powers and limitations? I think there
are good reasons to believe that they are not. In what ways, then,
could the present system be changed for the better?

III

Teaching Practice seen as a Developmental Process

As we have seen, students themselves express a desire for more
experience in the classroom. A group of second-year students
expressed the growing anxiety they felt about not knowing their
own abilities as teachers:

> We have been here a year and a half and we still don't really have any
> feel about whether we can or whether we will like teaching or not.
> Our only lengthy observation (3 weeks) we were giving tests and most
> of us did little or no teaching . . . it seems mad to come this far
> without finding out whether we have any abilities in what we wish to
> become.

Although these students had been going into school in half-
days and in small groups, the complaint, I felt, was a genuine

---

[14] See Iona and Peter Opie's *The Lore and Language of Schoolchildren* (Oxford
University Press).

one, and needed to be met. So, more teaching practice: but to say this is only to point to the area where more of our attention needs to be given. I believe it is *the conditions* of teaching practice that we ought to be examining — not merely their length or number. Do the colleges provide the best conditions for the students to realize the possibilities of creative teaching? Many students have expressed to me a deep uneasiness about knowing they are being visited in order to be assessed. Such anxiety is obviously destructive of adventurous teaching. Knowing that each lesson the supervisor watches is being consciously assessed and graded, the student excludes all those ideas which, because they are alive and still groping towards a definite shape, could well involve embarrassment or failure. Instead the student selects a closed structure which will achieve those certain classifiable 'results' he assumes the tutor will be impressed by. A tutor recently described to me a class where all the children were cutting out meticulously identical shapes to the well-formulated instructions of the student. The mass-production of beauty! The lesson provides a parody of the sort of 100 per cent safe teaching that the students resort to, under an understandable insecurity. Some tutors' interest in meticulous preparation on a set of immaculate notes and perfect diagrams further encourages and indeed, confirms, such mechanical teaching. Tutors ought to remember here that they are not evaluating the nation's book-keepers but potential teachers who will teach well in as much as they can bring ideas, facts, skills, intuitions, interpretations, to life in the thrusting, oscillating human community which is the classroom.

Clearly more teaching practice on these terms does not constitute an answer to the problems. But what are the alternatives?

I would like to make three suggestions, one for each of the three years of the students' course.

In addition to the three-week observation period in the first year, there should also be a prolonged period of time, perhaps four to six weeks in the second term, in which students become responsible for a small group of children inside the larger class. Such groups might be selected on a number of different criteria, e.g. some might be remedial groups, others mixed, others extremely able children. During this practice, the student, in relationship with his tutor and the teacher of the whole class, would be responsible for the work of this small group. Depending on the needs of the teacher, the student might be free to develop certain areas of activity on his own, while at other points he would be asked to work alongside the class teacher. What are the advantages of this scheme? I think, apart from merely providing more experience in schools, it also provides an altogether more gentle and useful initiation into the realities of the classroom. The student, for instance, is not in this way so terrified by a sea of unknown faces, knowing that he must take the responsibility for the complete syllabus, as well as the problem of over-all control. Yet he is far from being an idle observer, as often tends to happen on observation practice. With such a limited but definite commitment, the first-year student would be involved, I would suggest, to precisely the right degree. He is responsible for a small number of children whom he can get to know well as *individuals:* he has the freedom to experiment in certain defined areas: and he has also time to watch and evaluate the over-all structure of the classroom experience as well as the methods of the teacher.

The small group of pupils would provide a body of work which the student would be able to personally evaluate with a care which is almost impossible when given the larger numbers of a whole class. Such work — and the problems it raises in terms of assessment and development — could later be brought together and compared and explored in the professional courses. In this way in the first year, theory and experience, observation and participation, assimilation and experimentation could be pulled much more tightly together to the advantage of all: the students, the children, the school teachers and the lecturers.

In the second year the teaching practice should be concerned with the student making the step from teaching the small group to handling the whole class. I suspect that the insights gained in the first year into the individual child — who in the large classroom it is only too easy to forget — could here prove invaluable. But, again, we are asking too much if we expect the majority of students suddenly and successfully to take on the full role of the teacher. If we do, the chances are, that, out of fear and anxiety, he will resort to the dullest forms of teaching. Terrified to risk anything, to teach out of his enthusiasms, he will teach 'from the book to the bell'.

Here, I believe, in this intermediate year lies the responsibility of the tutor to collaborate and work with the student. The balance here must be delicate — and, if at the beginning ideas and suggestions derive more from the tutor, at the end they should be coming strongly from the student. It is important, also, that the tutor has the skill to recognize the particular style of teaching which the individual student may intuitively be working towards.

The notion, in fact, of neutrally watching and assessing a lesson is becoming, in the contemporary classroom, more and more meaningless. Behind it lurks the image of a teacher standing at the front ready to pour the gallons of imperious facts into the assembled empty vessels. As I have argued throughout this book, this image of learning is spurious and has been rejected in fact, by all the great educationalists from Plato (who said 'Avoid compulsion and let your lessons take the form of play') onwards. If the tutor is unwilling to teach with the student, to risk himself in this venture we call education by which we reach out to and continuously extend our frontiers of meaning and concern, then I do not see how he can help the student in the classroom.

Given this foundation in the first two years, the possibilities for teaching practice in the third year could be made more varied. It is not uncommon to find in primary and middle schools, a project approach to learning which draws on a team of teachers, and in the case of the middle school, different departments. Following in the wake of the experiments and developments, the colleges could create the following choices for students about to commence their third year teaching practice. Students could be asked to choose from the following options:

1. To teach on his own (as is the present practice).
2. To teach collaboratively with one other student.
3. To teach collaboratively with two other students.

Of course, careful preparation would be needed by those choosing the second and third options but the advantages that could attend such choices must be obvious. As a teacher of English I encouraged many children to write songs — songs which I could neither sing nor set to music, the themes of which suggested historical study as well as material for art, all of which I was not competent to develop. With limitations like these, limitations in knowledge, skill and enthusiasm, I was often unable to take the work through to its proper conclusions, unable to develop the work as fully as I would have liked. Students who can draw on each other's talents can clearly provide a much richer experience for the children. It is also obvious that students working together can gain by comparing their observations of particular children as well as by discussing why certain lessons may have failed. Such work, mature and challenging, could only be successful coming, as I suggest it should, towards the end of a more subtly structured three-year course.

A Concluding Note

At the moment, our Colleges of Education are too insulated from
society. Many lecturers feel they have escaped from the
frustrations and confusions of the classroom and are reluctant to
come too close to the schools. The resulting isolation, while it may
preserve academic dignity, is as deadening as it is unreal. If
colleges are to meet the crisis in meaning and identity I mentioned
earlier, they must become more open. They must be prepared to
work with the schools and learn from them. There must be much
more real exchange between lecturers, teachers and students.
Even this, though, may not be sufficient. I believe that Colleges of
Education should seek to become cultural centres: centres which
would represent a central core of values and meanings: centres to
which the surrounding communities would be drawn. Such a
suggestion will be dismissed by the new bureaucrats of our
educational system as impractical and idealistic, but I would
contend that without some such aspiration, education, as that
quest for personal and communal fulfilment, ceases—as it has
already done in so many large and dismal buildings erected
under the name of 'education' and 'expansion', without
philosophical foundation or aesthetic care.[15]

In this essay I have sketched in bold strokes the case for a
creative rather than an academic approach to the training of
teachers. I have suggested that Colleges of Education should
break away from the universities, establish their own centres and
develop their own methods of study, and their own disciplines. I
have argued that these disciplines should be collaborative in
spirit, phenomenological rather than theoretical, personal more
than impersonal. I want now to show how a specific course in
autobiography, to which I have already briefly referred, could
form an indispensable part of such work.

[15] The present policy of closing down the small Colleges of Education and expanding
only the large is, of course, on educational grounds (and these are the grounds we must
guard) utterly demented.

SEVEN

Autobiography, Existentialism and the Training of Teachers

Each mortal thing does one thing
and the same:
Deals out that being indoors each
one dwells;
Selves—goes itself; *myself* it
speaks and spells;
Crying What I do is me: for
that I came.

Gerard Manley Hopkins

I

In the past, it has been common practice for students on entering a College of Education or an Education department at a university, to be asked to reflect on their educational background as a personal preparation for the more impersonal studies of Psychology and Sociology which follow. I believe that such a practice harbours the seed of a great design, but that the conditions imposed by the timetable—two weeks in which to complete the memories and no time to collaboratively explore their implications and ramifications—have prevented the seed from germinating. As a result the practice has deteriorated to the level of another exercise. A moment's reflection about the intimate and creative nature of autobiography ought to tell us that such a momentous task cannot be properly tackled unless considerable time is allocated to it: and not only time, but also the possibility of extremely sensitive and tactful supervision. From my own experience with students writing their own autobiography, I would suggest that at least one term—with meetings every week, lasting a minimum of one hour, with groups not more than twelve in number — is essential if the project is to find its own particular shape and depth.

This in the busy framework of educational studies is a lengthy stretch of time. Many would consider it unjustified. If such a scheme in autobiography were being put forward at a staff meeting, many would argue that any time allocated to such personal elusive activity would be better used by disseminating to the students more from the ever-expanding fund of empirical knowledge provided by the social sciences. Others would argue that the time would be more profitably spent by introducing the students to the practical problems of the classroom, to the hard realities of education. Both critics, for different reasons, would indicate that to develop a course in autobiography would be to digress too far from the pressing issues of modern education.

What then is the value of students, who are preparing to be teachers, devoting so much time to reflecting on the formative influences on their lives and considering, with imaginative sympathy, the formative influences on other lives? To begin to elaborate an adequate answer to this question, I must first answer the criticisms expressed above. It is important to notice that the two counter proposals, while different in content — one is academic, the other practical — have a common assumption. One group demands more knowledge, the other more technique, but both assume that education is an act of multiplication by which more and more is done or known. And behind this numerical notion lurks a further assumption: that education can successfully take place without reference to the condition of the individual. And this, sure enough, is the way in which education is still viewed in many of our schools, colleges and universities. Education, it is insisted, is a matter of information, of mastering technique. It is the notion of education that Dickens attacked in *Hard Times* and which F. R. Leavis pointed attention to when in his lecture *English — Unrest and Continuity* he quoted the following excerpt from a letter to *The Times:*

> University work falls into two main categories — contributions to knowledge and communicating knowledge to students.

The same conception of education has been given a respectable sociological form by, among others, John Vaizey:

> Modern education affects the economy in a number of ways: not only does it increase the flow of skills, but it assists people to acquire new techniques. Moreover it tends to destroy the traditional attitudes

which so impede progress, and it links knowledge with methods of production.[1]

In the industrial society, as the factory mass-produces products so the schools and institutions of education mass-produce knowledge and techniques. The individual is reduced to the status of a passive vessel moving on a conveyor belt and being filled, at the same time, with useful knowledge and necessary techniques. The result in our schools and colleges is a deep inertia among the students: a mindless torpor—or, what might better be described as a pathology of boredom.

Given such a conception of the function of education it is exceedingly difficult to justify the work in autobiography I am advocating for Colleges and Departments of Education. But, of course, it would be equally difficult to defend the place of drama, art, poetry, music, religion, myth—indeed all those subjective disciplines which seek to articulate the inner realm and to develop the whole man. Given such a solid empirical conception of education, all forms of imaginative enquiry, all forms of symbolic articulation, become 'soft options', indulgences, events doomed to live on the fringe of things.

We need then a different educational premise: a premise resting on actualities while it allows for flight into possibilities: a truer and more generous premise. In challenging the prevalent utilitarian dogma of education as the acquisition of facts and know-how, it might be helpful to ask, first of all, *where* does education take place? It would seem to take place inside the person. That seems obvious enough and I doubt such an observation would stir any controversy. It is the individual who knows, who reasons, who asks, who expresses, who seeks or fails to do so. There is, couching it in a different form, no knowledge, no science, no symbolism, no art, outside of all those individual minds which constitute, and have constituted, the human race. To end human life, which means to annihilate *all individual lives,* would be to end education. This may appear to the reader unbearably obvious, even trite. Yet if we consider further the implications buried here, we may find ourselves moving towards a radically different conception of education from the one that is now so powerful. Indeed we may find ourselves coming very close to those interior truths and personal aspirations which, as I wish

[1] John Vaizey, *Education for Tomorrow* (Penguin).

to show later, make the writing of autobiography so rich an enterprise.

Let us begin by restating the proposition that education takes place inside the person in the following way: *just as the act of creativity presupposes a creator, so knowledge presupposes a knower.* In their primary state, creation and knowledge are not objects-in-the-world, not artefacts which can be studied or measured or reproduced, but acts of the *individual* mind wholly engaged in articulating the importance of a specific experience. I emphasize the word individual because the word suggests a pure domain unaffected by feelings or the drives of contingency, an unchanging palace of essences, but this we know, from the revelations of psycho-analysis and the arguments of existentialists, is not the case. Thought, in its primary state, is shot through with feeling and intentionality. Any study of the great philosophers reveals that thought is experienced as an adventure, 'a risk' in Socrates' words, a stretching of the whole person to extend the barriers of spiritual perception. And as the thought cannot be divorced from the thinker, so the philosophy (however abstract) is expressive of the particular disposition of the thinker and the times in which he lives. Thus the concerns of Socrates' dialogues are rooted in the Greek City States at the moment when the inherited mythology was beginning to lose its hold on the consciousness of man. The 'cogito ergo sum' of Descartes comes at the end of the mediaeval communal world-picture and at the beginning of the Renaissance. The assertion of Kierkegaard — 'truth is subjectivity' — explodes into the nineteenth century when Faith had become compromised and a fanatical belief in pure objectivity became dominant.

At this point I must quickly return to our banal starting point (that education takes place inside the person) for I hope we have reached a stage in the argument where we can see both what important truth lies dormant in the assertion but, also, where it may stand in need of qualification. We have seen that education cannot, meaningfully, take place outside of the assenting individual, but that individual, we have suggested, does not exist outside of the torrent of pressures — pressures of the family, the school, friends, neighbours, history — which constitute his outer world. Indeed from the moment of birth we are let loose on a rushing stream of sensations, and (very soon after that) signs, symbols and artefacts. To exist (ex-istere) is to find ourselves beyond ourselves, irredeemably out in a number of worlds that have their own rhythms and patterns and that are yet wound into one multitudinous experience, the experience of each existing individual. It is in individual experience — and only there — that the I and the many interacting worlds of Nature, Time, Relationships, History, come together in an intricate, creative, and largely unconscious manifold.

Our obvious proposition no longer seems so certain or so accurate. Rather than to repair it with a qualification — it may be better to cast anew, for in the category of experience, which is neither the objective universe nor the subjective self but the wedding of the two ('my world', 'your world') we arrive at the foundation we are seeking for the discipline of autobiography. It is instructive to note here the etymological root of the word 'experience'. Experience comes from the Latin world, *experientia* denoting *the act of trying*. The root meaning points us to one important truth about experience: it is *not,* as Locke and the empirical tradition would have us accept, passive. It is not made up of sense-impressions passively recorded on the retina of the eye and inscribed on the *tabula rasa* of the mind, for

> This, as Blake insists with all the force of the creative imagination, is to deny the essential creativeness of life, and to be committed, therefore, to repressing life itself. Perception, he insists in art and aphorism, is creative, and there is a continuity from the creativeness of perception to the creativeness of the artist.[2]

Experience, as is suggested by its etymological origin, is assertive, creative, intentional. Although we are thrown out into the world in which we move and have our being, we yet create and recreate in our experience our vision of this world. As Vico said, with aphoristic concentration, 'We can know nothing that we have not made'.

Education, then, building on these foundations, is that power within experience which seeks to develop, refine, increase and deepen those truths created by experience: and here, one has to quickly add, the experience of *this* person here, *that* person there. As a corollary to this, it follows that the enemies of education are to be associated with those powers which, for whatever reason — commercial, political, social — blunt, dessicate, corrupt or destroy the positive urges, the hidden longings enfolded in each man's response to the world. Paradoxically

[2] F. R. Leavis, *Nor Shall My Sword* (Chatto & Windus).

education, in its institutionalized form, can be the enemy of
education in its true form.

What I hope I have shown is that education is not primarily
concerned with the accumulation of facts and techniques but
rather with the expression and clarification of individual
experience. The centre of education resides in the individual. If
we are to achieve a genuinely human education we must return
again and again, to the person before us, the child, the
adolescent, the adult, the individual who is ready, however dimly
and in need of however much support, to adventure both further
out into his experience and further into it, who is ready, in some
part of himself to risk himself in order to become more than he
now is. The teacher, the tutor, can provide the conditions and the
support for such a journey—but the journey itself can only be
made by the assenting and autonomous individual.

We are now in a position to see the important value of the
discipline of autobiography in the training of teachers and to
counter the arguments of those who would dismiss such a course
as an indulgence or a mere trimming to decorate the hard centre
of the conventional syllabus. If the reader agrees that the source
of education must reside in the experience of the individual, then
a preoccupation with facts and techniques in our colleges and
departments of education not only misses the target but aims in
the wrong direction. A richer and more fitting approach would
seek, through creative understanding, to reveal the intimate
relationship between being and knowing, between existence and
education, between self and culture. Here we stand at the steps
leading to the act of autobiography—for how better to explore
the infinite web of connections which draws self and world
together in one evolving *gestalt* than through the act of
autobiography in which the student will recreate his past and
trace the growth of his experience through lived time and felt
relationships? What better way to assert the nature of true
knowledge than to set the student ploughing the field of his own
experience? In hunting out those truths that were so close to him
he did not notice them, may he not discover that 'education' is a
dusty and much-abused word to denote that action of the inward
spirit, by which, often with difficulty, one discovers who one is?

In his *Journals* Kierkegaard described the order of knowledge I
have been defending in this introduction as follows:

It is the divine side of man, his inward action which means

everything, not a mass of information; for that will certainly follow
and then all that knowledge will not be a chance assemblage, or a
succession of details, without system and without a focussing point.

True knowledge is existential knowledge. The act of autobiography, above all, reveals to the student the truth of this
proposition, and, in so doing, prepares him to become a
responsible and responsive teacher. Who is better equipped to
bring education alive than one who knows through his inmost
experience what education is? Having outlined briefly the
educational and philosophical basis for a course in autobiography, I would like now to consider more closely the nature
of the discipline it entails.

II

The central concern of all autobiography is to describe, evoke
and generally recreate the development of the author's
experience. It is probably in all cases an attempt to answer the
following conscious or half-conscious questions: Who am I? How
have I become who I am? What may I become in the future?
Autobiography is, thus, concerned with time: not the time of the
clock, but the time in which we live our lives, with its three tenses
of past, present and future. Autobiography, as an act of writing,
perches in the present, gazing backwards into the past while
poised ready for flight into the future.

The past tense is the most obvious tense of autobiography and
needs little elaboration here. Rousseau declares in his Confessions
'to know me in my advanced years you must have known me well
in my youth'. The deepest roots of our identity penetrate into the
forgotten depths of the past. Even Sartre, who insists in his
philosophy on the revolutionary freedom man has to determine
his identity, concedes in his autobiography:

> All the characteristics of the child, worn, defaced, humiliated,
> huddled in a corner and passed over in silence, have survived in the
> fifty-year-old man.

Indeed, autobiography, the intense recreation of the author's
past, reveals a deeper power than freedom in our lives: the power
of individuation. Edmund Gosse's *Father and Son* is fascinating
in this respect. The extraordinarily powerful pressures of his
background (and in particular, of his father) urged him, as a
child, to reduce life to a series of objects and facts which could be
tabulated, neatly and abstractly:

The system on which I was being educated deprived all things, human life among the rest, of their mystery. The 'bare-grinning skeleton of death' was to me merely a prepared specimen of that featherless, plantigrade vertebrate, 'homo sapiens'.

Yet, again and again, *Father and Son* reveals how the suppressed part of the child's psyche triumphantly asserts itself. Edmund finds 'an indescribable rapture' in the pages of a sensational novel which he discovers by chance lining the inside of a trunk. He has phantasies whereby he believes he can magically bring to life his father's clinical drawings of butterflies and birds. In the garden, mysteriously, he experiences a sudden illumination: 'there was a secret in this world and it belonged to me and to a somebody who lived in the same body with me'. The innate identity, the inward and essential character of the self, will find itself, even when the forces that circumscribe it are hostile and alien. Autobiography is the search backwards into time to discover the evolution of the true self.

At the beginning of this chapter, though, I stated that autobiography was poised for flight into the future. It may have struck the reader as strange to stress the future tense in a form of writing which is so palpably preoccupied with the past. And yet in the conclusions to autobiography one is invariably aware of this submerged concern with the immediate future boldly surfacing. A student, for example, who has courageously grappled with the burden of her own past, finishes her autobiography looking towards the horizons:

> My parents did not know me till that moment, but they do now. They helped me back to my feet, supported me on loving crutches. Perhaps my life would have been so much different if they had known me and I would not be what I am. Its too late to repair but it's early days to understand myself.

Here one senses both a sober acceptance of what has been together with a calm purposeful gazing into the future. Even in the act of remembering, present and future needs play a decisive role. In some students' work one is aware of a hesitancy, perhaps even a reluctance, about remembering past experiences:

> Although one doesn't realize it I suppose to a certain extent the present is dictated by the past . . .
> I suppose my early childhood must have been quite unsettled . . . Perhaps I like to imagine it that way!

The reluctance may be caused by the initial difficulty of remembering in the present, events that lurk dimly on the furthest edges of consciousness or seem, in reason's estimation, to be unutterably trivial. Yet it is true, as Stendhal discovered, that by concentration one can recall more and more of childhood experiences one had thought irretrievably lost. One memory invariably opens a door to another, taking the autobiographer further and further down the passage of time. (When students read excerpts from their work in progress, I have found that quite often one account of a childhood game or event will release in those who are listening a flow of memories till then lost.)

But the hesitant and uncertain tone of some students' autobiography may have another source which I would like briefly to discuss. In *Love and Will,* Rollo May asserts that we only remember those past events and inner feelings which we are capable, at that point in time, of assimilating into our personalities.

> We are . . . unable to give attention to something until we are able in some way to experience an 'I can' with regard to it . . . *Memory is a function of intentionality.* Memory is like perception in this respect; the patient cannot remember something until he is ready to take some stand toward it.

This is a most important observation and sheds particular light on why, in certain students' autobiographies, we detect a nervous evasiveness, an unwillingness to step into dangerous territory, a complex detour around some massively silent obstacle. This must be accepted and respected; it is not the task of the tutor to bludgeon memory where, for its own deep reasons, it is unwilling to go. The terms of each autobiography can only be provided by the individual student: the student should be urged to go only where he feels himself ready to go. But, at the same time, the tutor must be there to provide, should it be necessary, a support—for he, too, having made a similar journey into the self must know the difficulties that may lie in wait.

The autobiographer's memory, to adapt Rollo May's formulation, will be in the service of his own deeper intentionality. This means, in effect, that the student will be happy to recreate those memories which he is ready to take some stand towards. In practice, it means that a number of students, with their interest in educational ideals, will elect to confine their autobiographies to their schooling. This, as well as providing a

safely defined area for exploration into the nature of the evolving
self, constitutes an excellent preparation for teaching experience.
The gifted teacher is always able in his imagination to see the
classroom with the child's eye. The writing of autobiography
nurtures this power. In their writing, the students rediscover the
child's evaluation of his teachers. Consider for example the
following shrewd assessment of a teacher recalled in one student's
autobiography:

> Mr Taylor, harsh man, fond of the slipper and loud voice kept me
> subdued. I like writing but get carried away so that often I missed
> words (or letters) out in my eagerness. He was brutal to me over
> this — he liked to twist my hair where it was short around my ears and
> point at the offending omission while I writhed and apologised. At an
> open day for parents he smiled ingratiatingly and told Mum that
> 'Peter's only fault is his brain is quicker than his pencil but that's
> nothing to worry about'. I loathed him for his deceit.

Or consider the assumption a small child may have about the
underlying nature of the teacher as described in another
autobiography:

> I first articulated my opinion of teachers when I was about 6 or 7.
> Somehow I got into conversation with one of our teachers who was
> always very pleasant to me.
> — Why are you a teacher? I asked.
> — Oh, well, because I like children, she said, rather surprised.
> — But I thought teachers had to hate children.
> — Oh, no, you have to like children if you're to be a teacher.
> I was taken aback by the apparent illogicality of this remark.

Or the way in which a teacher's response may change a child's
innocent actions into not so innocent strategies:

> As long as I owned up and apologised to the persons involved there
> was no need for me to worry and I think this was the correct way to
> treat such cases. However, there was one teacher called Mr Wickham
> (who very quickly became 'Wickham Wackham') who treated my
> jangling physical co-ordination with some degree of wrath. He
> automatically assumed that to break something was a conscious and
> deliberate act. Such a person seems to push one from genuine
> clumsiness into calculated error.

Great advances in understanding and sympathy can be gained
by the collaborative consideration of the student's experiences of
schooling. From a strongly-felt personal basis, discussion can

profitably develop about the nature and practice of education, both as it was and as it might have been.

Yet, for many, such public discourse will only be *one* level of involvement, pertinent and valuable yet not the deepest. A considerable number of students will welcome the discipline of autobiography in the manner of an inward quest. These students are ready to remember, to recall and to integrate into their identity the whole confused substance of the past. They welcome this opportunity to escape, for a time, the endless demands, distractions, commitments of the outer world. They intuitively know that 'nothing can be sole or whole that has not been rent' and realize the truth recorded in AE's poem:

> In ancient shadows and twilights
> Where childhood had strayed,
> The world's great sorrows were born
> And its heroes were made.
> In the lost childhood of Judas
> Christ was betrayed.

These students know on impulse that education, in its richest contours, embraces the whole enigmatic stream of life and, in their own writing, work to gain hold of it. This is no simple matter:

> I don't expect this to be easy. I shall need to add to it continuously and hope that it represents something reasonable by the time it is finished. The beginning must be the most difficult of all to write—groping in the dark—later, when other people have talked and I have something to compare myself with, I might be able to rationalise.

The metaphor 'groping in the dark' conveys well the uncertain probing that characterizes the more ambitious auto-biography—the autobiography which is prepared to embrace or soberly acknowledge truths that, before the act of writing, seemed pressing yet murky and elusive. As the following passages show this is not 'easy' and may take the writer, where he is ready for such a confrontation, back to traumatic childhood experiences and early and late adolescent experiences:

> The child walked towards the door and turned the handle, quickly pushed open the door and shut it behind her. Looking neither to left nor right she marched sturdily towards the door that led to the stairs. She opened the door but as she turned to close it behind her, in the shaft of light from the hall she saw it, a long narrow wooden box. She

opened the other door and dashed quickly up the stairs to her bedroom. Once there she threw herself upon the bed, body heaving with emotion.

She got up and went to make a cup of coffee. Yes, that was the time when everything changed, the time when her brother died and she started turning into herself, a reserve which she realized now would always be an intrinsic part of herself.

I was lying in bed one night with my arms outside the blankets—they suddenly turned into chicken's legs, bony, scrawny,—*old*. Everyone seemed in a hurry to grow up at grammar school. I just wanted to go on being a child. I remember when I was about 11 being panicky about having to stop playing with dolls. I knew people would laugh at me if they found out, but I couldn't bear the thought of giving up forever my little phantasy world in which my dolls were so important. I remember walking to school with a group of friends—I was about 14—one of them was talking about Christmas, she wanted clothes, records, a record player. I said all I wanted was a new hutch for my rabbit, and they all laughed.

'Yes Dad, I'll let you know how I get on.' But I could not help but feel that the gulf between our lives was widening. How could I stop it? Was this not the process of growing up, should I turn away from the future before me, and return to a house and some people I had always known? Unconsciously we had reached that final cross-roads where our paths diverged. Out of touch, out of sight, we had taken each other for granted and it was too late for a re-evaluation of our personal relations.

In such writing the mind does not shy away from anything. As in tragedy 'it does not protect itself with any illusion, it stands uncomforted, unintimidated, alone and self-reliant'.[3] And, curiously, it is often followed with a feeling of liberation—even joy:

I find, in spite of never having talked to this intensity in a group situation that I can follow people's flow, trains of thought. Am delighted, in Leeds I was thick academically. And I had always to feel inferior, quite irrationally. Now I go away exhilarated even if it has seemed an unresponsive afternoon. I am always reworking, always thinking, none of it is ever futile.

Such are the creative moments, pressing into the future which autobiography, as I have argued in this section, is poised ready to

[3] I. A. Richard's description of tragedy in *Principles of Literary Criticism* (Routledge & Kegan Paul).

fly into. Here, indeed, the way back is the way forward and the reward, if it can be reached, an enhanced affirmation of the self. For a few students not only plough the field of their experience they are also able to seed it for a harvest that may be theirs tomorrow. This, I would argue, is the deepest achievement made possible for the student of education through the discipline of autobiography.

III

The discipline of autobiography which I am advocating is primarily an inward and creative discipline centred on the related acts of reflecting on an re-creating the personal past. It is not academic. It begins and ends with what is given in experience. And yet it is of more than casual interest to see how the autobiographical form of writing has developed—for here, too, in our cultural past we discover the roots of our identity penetrating further back than we had imagined. In confronting St Augustine's *Confessions* we find ourselves at unexpected points, gazing at our own reflection. We encounter in St Augustine's autobiography that trembling and sustained inwardness which is one of the marks of Western Man and which derives from the powerful influence of the Hebraic religion on his being.

But why, we need to ask, hadn't the form of autobiography emerged before St Augustine? Why hadn't the Greeks, who had developed and perfected so many symbolic forms created autobiography? Matthew Arnold in *Culture and Anarchy* provides us with a clue to the answer when he describes the characteristic disposition of Hellenic man:

> To get rid of one's ignorance, to see things as they are, and by seeing them as they are to see them in their beauty, is the simple and attractive ideal which Hellenism holds out before human nature—, and from the simplicity and charm of this idea, Hellenism, is invested with a kind of aerial ease, clearness and radiancy: they are full of what we call sweetness and light. Difficulties are kept out of view, and the beauty and rationalness of the ideal have all our thoughts.

It was just such an informing belief in lucid reason which urged the Greeks to look for fixed and permanent truths, eternal essences, outside of the inward flux of his own mixed and contrary experience. So absolute was the belief in reason that for Aristotle it came to define man's essential nature. In his *Ethics* he observed:

What is naturally proper to every creature is the highest and pleasantest for him. And so, to man, this will be the life of Reason, since Reason is, in the highest sense, a man's self.

It is true that the power of reason is one of the defining characteristics of man's nature, yet, at the time, reason follows the line which leads from the specific to the abstract, from the existential to the essential. Reason transports the individual out of his own life and time and surroundings and houses him in logical necessities and radiant ideals. For Plato, ideas were luminous and eternal while existence was dark and mortal. Given such a dominant assumption, it is not surprising that no true form of autobiography emerged in Greek culture, for what the autobiographer relishes: the intimate texture, the fleeting impression, the flash of light at the end of a dim corridor, the fragrant smell which haunts the mind, in fact, all those memories which take the writer spiralling inwards, is what the Greek mind would have dismissed as second-order reality, ephemeral illusions, insignificant shadows unworthy of the attention of a great writer or thinker. Because the deep and problematic nature of experience was not considered a primary reality, any great act of autobiography, in which the writer plunges into his own multitudinous and unique existence, was rendered impossible. In his book, *Design and Truth in Autobiography* Roy Pascal states the case quite simply by declaring that in Greek and Roman civilization —

> never was the unique personal story in its private as well as public aspect considered worthy of single-minded devotion of the author.

It was, thus, left to St Augustine, at the time of the dissolution of the Roman Empire, to write the first deep autobiography. Again in his book, Roy Pascal pinpoints the essential quality that made the *Confessions* spiritually and artistically different from any writing which had preceded it.

> Out of memory he [St Augustine] re-collects the scattered pieces of his personality, not in order to demonstrate himself as an Aristotelian entelechy, perfected from the beginning: not like Marcus Aurelius to construct a basic model: but to show his spiritual evolution, the coming-into-being of his full personality — a process of such startling change that he must ascribe it to Divine intervention . . .
> Deeds are not recounted because they occurred, but because they represent stages of spiritual growth.

In the phrase 'spiritual evolution' Roy Pascal defines the essential quality of the *Confessions*. The notion of evolution, of rational development, would not have been alien to Greek civilization—but the notion of spiritual, with the connotations of febrile inwardness that Augustine gives to it, certainly would have. The spiritual dimension, which Augustine's introspective intellect habitually inhabits, comes not from the Greek but from Hebraic culture. Here in the conflict between two cultures we discover, I believe, one of the reasons why Augustine was the first man to write a true autobiography.

In St Augustine the Hebraic stream of Faith and the Hellenic stream of Reason met and the confluence was as productive as it was turbulent. When such great contraries are drawn together, psychic tension is engendered which if it does not destroy the individual mind (for ideas only live in individual minds) is creative of new vision. In St Augustine's *Confessions,* though not in his theology which develops within the Greek framework, man is hurled by his dark and passionate nature beyond the order of knowledge and the control of the will. The ancient unity of the Greeks, depending on the all-embracing energy of the intellect, is irreparably broken, for in Augustine *we are always more than we can know.* 'There is', declares St Augustine, 'in man an area which not even the *spirit of man* knows of'. And again: 'There is in me a lamentable darkness in which my latent possibilities are hidden from myself, so that my mind, questioning itself upon its own powers, feels it cannot rightly trust its own report'. In confronting such a limitation to knowledge, the essential questions of philosophy became introspective and existential. The question asked by the Greeks '*What* is man?' was transformed into the more pressing question '*Who* is man?' And with the asking of the question, new acts of human attention were made possible, new areas of consciousness discovered. One of these acts of attention was autobiography which allowed a writer to explore nakedly and without apology the uncharted territory of himself. The *Confessions* are, as Peter Brown rightly says in his biography of Augustine, 'a manifesto of the inner world',[4] a turning away from the mechanical and public to the beauties and dangers of the inward soul.

The question 'Who am I?' which draws existentialist philosophy and autobiography together, also had, I suspect, another source. The radical question erupted in the mind of the

---

[4] Peter Brown, *Augustine of Hippo* (Faber & Faber).

responsive individual at that point in history when the
continuation of man was felt to be uncertain. The *Confessions*
were written during the fifth century when the Roman
Empire was in a state of rapid and seemingly irresistible
dissolution. We discover in Augustine's writing the image of a
society which has degenerated into a besotted mob craving for
ever more violent and bloody spectacles. Augustine's comments
on his friend Alipius who was, before his conversion, pulled into
the whirlpool of corrupt fashion, burn into the reader and, at the
same time, portray the vicious undercurrents let loose by a
civilization in decline:

> For as soon as he beheld that blood (the blood of Christians in the
> amphitheatre) he drank down with it a kind of savageness; he did not
> now turn away but fastened his gaze upon it, and drinking up the cup
> of fury ere he knew it, he became enamoured with the wickedness of
> those combats, and drunk with a delight in blood. He was no more
> the Alipius who had come there, but one of the common herd with
> which he came, and an entire companion of those that led him.
> What shall I say more? He gazed, he shouted, he burned with the
> desire of it, and he carried home from thence such a measure of
> madness as provoked him to return, not only with them by whom he
> was formerly debauched, but more earnestly than they even going so
> far as to seduce others also.

In those periods when the configuration of inherited meanings,
values, aspirations have either become corrupt or devoid of
vitality, the responsive individual is compelled, by the power of
his personality reacting to the times, to search out a vision of man
which transcends the mediocrity or savagery around him. Fifteen
centuries after Augustine, Kierkegaard and Nietzsche found
themselves outside Christendom for Christianity in the nineteenth
century had become complacent, hypocritical and lost in the
daily pressures of what Blake called 'single vision'. It was their
turn to face Christianity, the religion which St Augustine had so
passionately embraced and disseminated, with the same radical
question (Who is man?) and the same inward desire for spiritual
transformation. It is also pertinent here to quote from the
introduction to Herbert Read's gentle autobiography written in
the middle of our own century:

> The death wish that was once an intellectual fiction has now become
> a hideous reality and mankind drifts indifferently to self-destruction.

To arrest that drift is beyond our individual capacities, to establish one's individuality is perhaps the only possible protest.[5]

The impulse to write derives from the desire to enrich one's identity *against* the destructiveness of the age. A negative age drives the creator inwards. In Van Gogh's intensely disturbing and unflinchingly honest self-portraits one discovers again, the truth of this assertion. 'The madness of the circus' to use Augustine's words, drives the individual into himself to forge an inner sequence of meanings where the outer ones have collapsed. Against the brutal and the banal, the creator goes in quest of those transcendent energies without which no human life can survive long.

Nietzsche declared in *Thus Spake Zarathustra:* 'One must have chaos within one to give birth to a dancing star'. His illuminating epigram takes us one step further into answering our question: why did autobiography begin in the fourth century in Western civilization? There was, as we have seen, in St Augustine's time, chaos without; but in the *Confessions* one senses more than this: one is made powerfully aware of chaos exploding within. It is St Augustine's own personality, in his guilts, in his forebodings, in his lusts, aspirations, anxieties, hopes, that one detects that chaos which, perhaps most of all, helped to give birth to the dancing star of autobiography. St Augustine's trembling emotions cannot, it is true, be divorced from the two forces we have already delineated: the confluence of Reason and Faith; the turmoil of the period; and yet the reader of the *Confessions* senses a stormy energy beyond these which can only be located at the centre of Augustine's own personality.

William James in his classic study *The Varieties of Religious Experience* defines brilliantly the temperament of St Augustine. It will be remembered that William James distinguished between the temperament of the 'first born' and that of the 'twice-born'. The former, he writes:

> . . . are born with an inner constitution which is harmonious and well-balanced from the outset. Their impulses are consistent with one another, their will follows without trouble the guidance of their intellect, their passions are not excessive, and their lives are little haunted by regrets.

Whereas the 'twice-born' are persons

[5] Herbert Read, *The Contrary Experience* (Secker & Warburg).

whose existence is little more than a series of zig-zags, as now one tendency and now another gets the upper hand. Their spirit wars with their flesh, they wish for incompatibles, wayward impulses interrupt their most deliberate plans, and their lives are one long drama of repentance and effort to repair misdemeanours and mistakes.

Later on in the same chapter entitled significantly *The Divided Self* William James adds to this description declaring that:

> The man's interior is a battle-ground for what he feels to be two deadly hostile selves, one actual, the other ideal.

There can be no doubt that Augustine, in every respect, belongs with the twice-born. His life, as revealed in his autobiography, is out of harmony: a constant prey to haunting emotions, irrational impulses, deep transcendental longings. Again and again, the *Confessions* sketch a world that is elusive, enigmatic and paradoxical:

> And if any prosperity smiled upon me, it grieved me to apprehend it, because, almost before I could close my hand upon it, it fled away.

> I became unto myself an enigma, and I would ask my soul why it was sad, and why it inflicted me so vehemently, yet it could make no answer.

> While I thus desired a happy life, I yet feared to seek it in its true abode, and I fled from it while yet I sought it.

These lyrical formulations of inner discord characterize the *Confessions* and reveal why it was that St Augustine, in an age in which the daily surface of life was splintering into a thousand parts, was the first man driven to write the history of his own identity.

The lucidity of rational knowledge had provided an escape-route from those truths, those visions, those dreams, those fathomless desires stirring strangely within. With St Augustine, through the instrument of autobiography, man once again sought to return to those primary sources of Being which the excessive cultivation of Reason and the turning of the community into a mob-collectivity had done so much to obscure.

St Augustine is commonly known as one of the founding fathers of the Christian Church: but for us, as teachers and writers, he should perhaps be better known as the father of autobiography and existentialism.

In St Augustine's *Confessions* my two main concerns in this essay, the act of autobiography, the nature of existential truth, come together. William Barret's analysis of St Augustine in his book *Irrational Man* crystallizes the central argument I am making and I would, therefore, like to quote from it at length:

> The existentialism of St Augustine lies in his power as a religious psychologist, as expressed most notably and dramatically in his *Confessions*. Augustine had almost a voluptuous sensitivity to the Self in its inner inquietude, its trembling and frailty, its longing to reach beyond itself in love; and in the *Confessions* he gives us a revelation of subjective experience such as even the greatest Hellenic literature does not, and could not, because this interiorisation of experience came through Christianity and was unknown to the earlier Greeks. Where Plato and Aristotle had asked the question What is man? St Augustine (in the *Confessions*) asks Who am I? — and the shift is decisive. The first question presupposed a world of objects, a fixed natural and zoological order, in which man was included. Augustine's question . . . implies that man cannot be defined by being located in that natural order, for man, as the being who asks himself Who am I? has already broken through the barriers of the animal world. Augustine thus opens the door to an altogether different view of man than had prevailed in Greek thought.

Thirteen-and-a-half centuries were to pass before the next great autobiography was triumphantly (and somewhat indulgently) to enter the same door and enter the labyrinthine caverns of the self. Rousseau's *Confessions*, written in 1765 and published in 1781, proclaimed in another Age of Reason the formative powers of the emotions in the regulating of human life. Rousseau's long and passionate book was to usher in the age of autobiography. In the following decades many of the major writers: Goethe, Wordsworth, Coleridge, Mill, Gosse, Ruskin, Trollope, Tolstoy, Gorki, were to turn back to their childhood for sustenance, understanding and inspiration.

IV

The most demanding work for the student engaged in the discipline of autobiography will remain the individual attempt to grapple with his past experience. Many will find this difficult. They will find themselves, perhaps for the first time in their education, facing a series of problems (about what to include, what to exclude, how to begin) which are inherently personal. The tutor can suggest possibilities but he cannot and should not seek to solve the student's dilemmas. And the student must remain at all times free to reject the proffered suggestions.

The tutor's main task I would argue, is often to clarify what is simply implicit in the student's experience through a series of questions. At the beginning of one tutorial in which the students were gathering to read for the first time excerpts from their first drafts, one mature student looked up and said:

'Does it have to be personal?'

'How do you mean?' I asked.

'I mean written in the first person', she said.

'Gorki's autobiography was written in the third person', I answered.

That was enough. The student took out her writing pad and scrawled for a few minutes. Then she read out what she had written.

> Her earliest memories consisted of short, brief, bright pictures: tea bushes, coolies, brilliant flowers, heat, all merging into a canvas of flat colour. The first concrete memory, incorporating picture, sound and emotion did not come until about three and a half years old. That memory did not need extracting from a whole, it was complete in itself. White—white shorts, white shirt, white socks. She'd demanded that he wear white, as she remembered him, but had forgotten how huge he was. Still, the thought of the surprise they had brought overcame her awe and, grabbing his hand, she dragged him to the cabin. Pointing to a cot on the bunk she said, 'Daddy, look what we've brought you.'

The student had suddenly found that she could best capture her childhood by employing a third-person narrative. For some reason, an impersonal method of writing released her imagination and freed her memory which until then had been constricted by the direct first-person presentation we normally associate with autobiography. Another student, without prior discussion, intuitively used the third-person to convey (and also to distance) the more harrowing experiences of his past and used the first-person narrative to evoke the more leisurely and happy moments. In every case, the form chosen, the style used, is expressive of the person writing and constitutes an essential part of the autobiography. The tutor may provoke, question, compare and contrast, but, in the end, the student, the autobiographer, must decide *how* he will write and *what* must be his proper subject matter.

Where, then, does the study of the tradition of

autobiography—the study, for example, of St Augustine, Rousseau, Mill and Gorki—come in? I think there are two ways in which the tutor can draw on this material.

First of all he can regard it as a secondary source of autobiographical material which he can introduce, where needed, to deepen or amplify or interpret the turmoil of experience thrown up in his student's work. Let me give one example. A student expressing a moment of illumination in her childhood, wrote:

> About halfway along the road to adulthood I went through a very strange experience. A psychiatrist could probably explain it away in a few well chosen words. It baffled me. At seven I had the sudden and world shattering realization that I was a human being, an individual, responsible to and for myself. Only I could think my thoughts, I was not a part of the adults around me. This revelation was at once exciting and terrifying. What would happen to me if my mother died? Should I have to go into a home? How does one arrange a funeral?

Such an experience could gain by being sympathetically compared to those experiences of 'being I' that Gosse records in his *Father and Son* or to Jung's description in his autobiography *Memories, Dreams, Reflections* of becoming self-conscious:

> I was taking the long road from school from Klein-Huningen, where we lived to Basel, when suddenly for a single moment I had the overwhelming impression of having just emerged from a dense cloud. I knew all at once: now *I am myself!* It was as if a wall of mist were at my back, and behind that wall there was not yet an 'I'. But at this moment *I came upon* myself. Previously I had existed too, but everything had merely happened to me. Now I happened to myself. Now I knew: I am myself now, now I exist. Previously I had been willed to do this and that: now I willed. This experience seemed to me tremendously important and new: there was 'authority' in me.

To introduce Gosse's and Jung's autobiography at this particular point would be to confirm the student's own uncanny realization of self and, in the context of the seminar, to make such an experience a more accessible part of our human reality.

Secondly, the great autobiographies can be considered on their own terms. The tutor, if he wishes to embark on such a study can best decide when the students will gain most from it. Clearly some autobiography could be introduced in this manner as a means of beginning the whole project. Here Gorki's *My Childhood* and Herbert Read's *The Contrary Experience* being so direct and so lyrically powerful provide excellent starting points. A more detailed consideration of autobiography—including a discussion of the philosophical issues I raised earlier—is probably best reserved until after the student's own work is completed.

I would like, finally, to clarify a number of points.

In the discussion periods which I suggested earlier should take place once a week and last a minimum of one hour, I invited each student to read an excerpt from his own autobiography which, at that point, was in process of being written. Some students read only a few excerpts from their work. Others choose to read, week by week, their whole script. Here the tutor's influence must be subtle and indirect. Any compulsion is alien to the liberating spirit of autobiography. By his presence the tutor must be able to create the feel of trust: that trust in which each student feels able to present himself, to be who he is. If this spirit of trust and collaboration can be established, the weekly meeting becomes an essential focus to the work. The meeting provides the private act of autobiography with a valuable public face. The student knows he is not plunging into himself alone. He is doing it with others, and often, at the meetings, he is gaining as much from their descent as his own. The mutuality engendered need not be explicit. It is most powerful and real where it is tacit and assumed: for as one student pointed out—

'There is a certain amount of honesty among us that might be lost if we analyse our reactions too much.'

After such a course in autobiography, the student, having had time in which to find his own centre, and to have refined his own conception of education, is inwardly prepared to move outwards to the critical study of educational philosophies and theories. For this reason, and for the other reasons I have given earlier in this chapter, it would seem to me that a course in autobiography, at once practical and creative, provides an essential beginning to the sensitive training of teachers.

In this chapter, as in the preceding three chapters, I have been primarily concerned with the practice of teaching, with actual methods and their underlying principles. Yet education as an activity takes place within society. It is impossible and undesirable for education to retreat very far from that society. The school should not be an enclave, a retreat from life: it should be at the centre of the community as was the medieval Church. And yet, as we have seen, the values of education differ and are at war with those of the mass consumer-society. Education would nurture a desire for truth, for individuality, for sensitive relationship, for creativity. The mass society would inculcate conformity, passivity, inertia, cynicism, egoism. The conflict between these two unequal forces is deep and irreconcilable. The English teacher, committed both to inward and historic truths, knows he is a member of a tiny minority, articulate but largely powerless. What can he do? What can those teaching the subjective disciplines do? What can the schools, colleges and universities do? Is it possible to draw up a politics based on educational and cultural principles? A politics which places man, the *animal symbolicum,* at the centre of the frame?

It is to these questions, and the problems which they raise, that I now wish to turn.

PART III

Politics

A power can be overthrown only by another power.

Spengler

EIGHT

The Politics of the Imagination

Any system built on the passiveness of the mind must be false.

Coleridge

. . . wisdom first speaks in images.

W. B. Yeats

We want the creative faculty to imagine that which we know: we want the generous impulse to act that which we imagine: we want the poetry of life: our calculations have outrun our conception: we have eaten more than we can digest.

Shelley

T. S. Eliot claimed in his *Notes Towards the Definition of Culture:* 'for the immediate future, perhaps for a long way ahead, the continuity of culture may have to be maintained by a very small number of people indeed — and these not necessarily the best equipped with worldly advantages'. After a quarter of a century Eliot's prediction still holds good though his calm, stoic, resignation is at variance with our present frayed experience of a world ending. 'The immediate future', 'a long way ahead' — unlike Eliot, we are unable to imagine the shape of tomorrow and the expanse of time stretching behind tomorrow is beyond all human conception. We are unable even to conceive of, to conceptualize, to symbolize the immediate reality before us, the reality, which of all realities ought to be uniquely ours.

It seems to me that man no longer attains to speech. There is a violence in things which becomes a violence in its own right and prohibits speech. A violence stronger than the word. Things change: they hinder our efforts to name them, and therefore our efforts to establish order through naming, to allow others the ensuing benefit . . . Perhaps it's evidence of an apocalyptic world in which man lives with the possibility of destroying himself . . . It's certain that, no longer able to imitate or inherit the past, we have lost the knowledge of things.[1]

The words are Guiseppe Ungaretti's.

'A continuity of culture': some threads which we can draw out from the past into the present which, as it unfolds, draws in, implicates, the future: with life to create a design, a tapestry, where the strands and colours interweave to form one image, one beauty: certainly that is what is required. Yet what a strange dream it is, in the latter part of the twentieth century, when scientists no longer understand science but the merest fraction, a specialized division of an already specialized subdivision of the whole: when artists are urged to discard both outward tradition and inward compulsion in the name of fashions artificially fostered and artificially perpetuated; when philosophers no longer talk of wisdom or psychologists of the psyche but merely offer further methods of analysis and treatment; when in every sphere of life, the harsh process of abstraction and division accelerates to a speed we are helpless to control. What a time to dream the dream of culture, to inwardly see the tree of knowledge, its root and blossom one. Yet it is through an encounter with such extremes, between imaginative possibility and confused reality, through a dialectic of opposites conducted not so much in the market place but more often in the deep recesses of the imagination, that change, issuing from a changed consciousness, is destined to come. Initially such a change might not differ in content from Eliot's view of the future depending on a cultured minority who, without advantages and spurning luxuries, resist the debased standards of life about them. But its quality will differ from that of Eliot's, it will be neither stoical nor resigned; rather it will, because the times are critical, burn with an energy fierce and implacable.

I have used Eliot's phrase 'continuity of culture', yet the word culture stands in need of elucidation. Eliot suggests that the word can be used simply to describe 'that which makes life worth living'. But *what* makes life *worth* living? It is surely possible to invent a society—it would not, I am afraid, require too much invention—in which the bulk of present liberal and socialist principles would be fully realized: let us say, a society which has eradicated poverty, which had distributed goods justly, which

---

[1] Ungaretti. From 'On Estranged Words and Michaux's Dream of the Universe and perhaps mine', *Agenda*, Vol. 8, No. 2. Spring, 1970.

had made equal education available for all, which from birth to death administered to all the complex demands of human life, and yet in which life would not be worth living.[2] It would be a society in which organized reason had usurped the place of individual excellence (with its necessary corrollary of individual evil). Indeed, in such a society, it would be possible to view the act of suicide as a positive gesture, as the last and extreme assertion of transcendent identity, a perverse act spelling human dignity. Such a society, while possessing a complicated network of entertainment — yes, and all manner of means for therapy — would still be devoid of culture in Eliot's sense of the word. It would be a society which, against all appearances, essentially deprived the individual of that peculiar and problematic experience of I, of I existing, feeling, willing, choosing. And culture, it seems to me, is the response, not necessarily conscious, to this disturbing/elating/oscillating experience of I existing, the response forming a transcendence of the self through expression and creation. And it is this uniquely human experience, with all its diverse manifestations, which makes life worth living.

Such a conception of culture, unlike that of sociologists, is *qualitative:* it is seen to consist of all that which promotes and perfects a distinctive style of life, an inner constellation of values, aspirations and beliefs which are given form and transmitted to others in action, in gesture, in word, in deed. Yet to emphasize, as I so far have done, the individual and to limit society from the account would be grossly misleading. If culture is concerned with the shaping and refining of the inward man yet it can in no way be confined to him; for the very media (language, sign and symbol) through which he is able to discover and project his style of life are social gifts. And beyond this, an individual style of life cannot be sustained, will inevitably disintegrate under the ceaseless frettings of anxiety, unless it be sustained by a sympathetic community, however small. When such a milieu is missing, suicide (not necessarily in its literal form — there are many ways of dying) becomes a negative expression of identity.

[2] In listing the changes that Socialists and Liberals would like to see, equal education, fair distribution of goods etc., I have, inevitably, in the back of my mind an image of Swedish society — a society which the Liberal Press always refers us to for its enlightened policies. The suicide rate in Sweden is very high. It is more than possible that the rate of suicide is in direct relationship to the amount of socially enlightened legislation and organization. Could it be that the person is too tightly confined; that all those possibilities in man which transcend society are severely frustrated; and that suicide is an expression of this situation?

Even Rousseau who, in his ideal scheme of education, withdrew Emile from the corrosive influences of society, decided to educate Sophie to form his ideal partner: while Rousseau himself, to support his own anxious identity, invented a community of uncorrupted primitive beings with whom he identified and from whom he received inner sustenance. And since the time of Rousseau, writers of all dispositions have tended to find buttresses for their implosive visions in past communities. Ruskin and Carlyle located their society in medieval Europe; Lawrence in Etruscan civilization before it was destroyed by the great mechanical Empire of Rome; Pound turned partly to traditional Chinese society with its Confucian wisdom: Yeats in 'The Tragic Generation' dated the period which embodied his ideals:

> Somewhere about 1450, though later in some parts of Europe by a hundred years or so, and in some earlier, men attained to personality in great numbers, 'Unity of Being', and became like a 'perfectly proportioned human body', and as men so fashioned held places of power, their nations had it too, prince and ploughman sharing that thought and feeling.

In Yeats' chosen period—as in other epochs of harmonious living—the individual is not seen in opposition to the community, but as the valuable differentiated expression of the general animating energy, the vivid flower gracing the dense tree. Nor are the values, beliefs and aspirations abstract fabrications, but segments of an encompassing life wisdom which manifests itself at all levels of society and in a complex hierarchy of artefacts, from a rich fardel of stories to the tiles round the chimney pieces, from paintings and music to the hangings that keep back the draught.[3]

Culture is thus a densely imbricated pattern which, although partly inherited, has, if it is to live, to be constantly reworked and recreated by each generation. And it is the effort of re-making which nurtures and satisfies the two complementary needs of man, the need to *belong* and the need to *be,* the bright assertion of active identity.

It is central to my theme that the various Romantic visions of a past community are all prior to the eighteenth century, for the eighteenth century marks the crucial transition from a mythopoeic response to a scientific response. During the

---

[3] I am, of course, here referring to Yeats' aspiration as expressed in *The Trembling of the Veil:* 'I wished for a world, where I could discover this tradition perpetually, and not in pictures and in poems only, but in tiles round the chimney piece and in the hangings that kept out the draught'.

eighteenth century, image and knowledge were finally severed, and knowledge, split from the imagination and the feelings, gained a powerful ascendancy which has continued, largely unquestioned, into our own times. Kenneth Clark in *Civilisation* suggests the manner of this dramatic change in a comment on Newton and the eighteenth-century scientists:

> They continued to use a celestial globe in which the constellations were grouped in the form of men and animals: they continued to accept the kind of personification that one gets on the ceiling of the Painted Hall. But all the same, they recognised that all these were fancies, that reality lay elsewhere, in the realm of measurement and observation. And so began the division between scientific truth and imagination . . .[4]

Reality, for the eighteenth-century scientist lay not in images (which, divorced from intellect became objects of piety) or in the imagination (which had to be rigidly excluded from scientific procedure) but in the precise and impersonal measuring of the external world. Religion and art, as living powers providing the comprehensive symbols of society, effectively ended at that point in time and consciousness. Montesquieu, visiting England in 1730, observed:

> There is no religion in England. If anyone mentions religion, people begin to laugh.

From the eighteenth century forward we can trace the progressive rise of the scientific method, a growing insistence on verification, quantification and collaboration, with the consequent decline of the religious, the relentless pushing of poetic and metaphysical forms of knowledge, like stale rags, into the very corners of social life. At the same time, and in intimate dependent relationship, we can observe the violent movement of the industrial revolution, the rapid growth in population and organization, in production and consumption. And now, in the latter half of the twentieth century, in the great industrial powers, in Russia, in America, in Europe, we are witnessing a further stage of development, a transition from gritty industrialism to smooth technocracy. This complex development involves the progressive merging of small units into large, a growing emphasis on expertise, management and methods of psychological

---

[4] The Painted Hall that Kenneth Clark refers to is at the Royal Hospital, Greenwich, London.

manipulation, and the steady emergence of a new class, the rise of
the man who carries computer paper, the middle man, the
bureaucrat. And the whole system (not, as Marcuse has pointed
out, *essentially changed*) is precariously held together by an ethic
which recognizes no moral imperatives beyond 'economic
viability' and the 'march of progress'. I have said that it is now
impossible to symbolize or conceptualize our society—I am sure
that this is true—but as far as this drift into technocracy is
concerned, Kafka has provided an accurate image in his novel
The Castle, where the anonymous K. wanders through an
institution in which life and responsibility for life is endlessly
deferred. Ours is a society in which the growth of identity—the
growth of culture—is made not only difficult but, to judge by the
number of suicides, schizophrenics, addicts and limp 'drop-outs',
perilous.

In considering the present discord between the individual and
society, the argument could turn in many directions. I must
restrict myself to my main concerns, poetry and education—and
the language on which they both depend. What effect did the
scientific and industrial revolution have on language? It is
through language that we become aware of society and of
ourselves in society. The assumptions that a language embodies
exert a decisive influence on understanding. Our evaluation of
events, and even the events themselves, are largely determined by
the nature of the words which society has made available to
us. Again, words have peculiar powers over us because their
influence tends to work at an unconscious level. We do not realize
that often it is the received pattern of words which commits us to a
particular viewpoint. It is a saddening fact that many words in
common usage today implicitly debase the imaginative faculty.
The words myth, fable, story, tale are used commonly by both the
mass media and schools to indicate deception and falsehood.
Thus in *The Times:* 'one of the great myths of our time is that
European farming is something carried on by inefficient, if
picturesque, peasants'. It is not surprising to find that our society
has relegated the traditional forms of life wisdom, the fairy story,
the myth, the legend, to the nursery. Nor is it surprising to find
that we invariably employ such terms as 'highly subjective' or
'highly emotive' to disparage, while the converse terms, 'highly
objective' or 'highly rational' are used to indicate all but
unconditional praise. Phrases like these, common in educated
speech, which embody the assumptions and judgements of three

hundred years of unquestioned scientific advance, in effect, deny the powers of the imaginative and passionate energies.

As early as 1667, Sprat in his *History of the Royal Society* wrote, 'poetry is the parent of superstition'. According to Mill, Bentham, who believed that every flicker of life was susceptible to measurement, thought that 'words . . . were *perverted* from their proper office when they were employed in uttering anything but precise logical truth'. It has been a commonplace of twentieth-century philosophy that only verifiable statements are meaningful and that other forms of language belong to the realms of private nonsense. For three centuries the main intellectual and economic drive of our civilization has attempted to strip down metaphor, to pull down the creative symbol and to replace it with the precise sign. The obsession with verification and the language of verification permeates our society. Thus, for example, it is characteristic to find an author claiming in a recent popular book on the universe:

> The views of Plato on astronomy typified both the confusion and the open-mindedness of the times. At the beginning of his philosophic career, he imagined that the gods drove shining chariots across the sky. Later he wondered whether the earth was flat or round.[5]

What is so damaging here is the identification of the poetic with confusion, and of the scientific with openmindedness. Yet there is no *confusion* in seeing the sun as a dazzling chariot drawn by the gods: it is a vast and imaginative conception which expresses delight in creation and excites and satisfies the whole mind. To discount such a vision, to reduce it to mental confusion, is to deny all those complex and creative powers in man which do not conform with the limited preoccupations of scientific enquiry. This rejection of the imagination is happening all the time. As a result we have a mass of educated people who, when reflecting on the substance of their lives, employ a language which is dry and abstract and utterly devoid of resonance and depth. The language of the educated today is like a thin but impenetrable skin sealing off whatever depth might lie below. The language arrives in given shapes, connects mechanically and is so remote from the hurly-burly of actual experience it compels us to split theory from practice, thought from feeling, conception from existence. Charles Parker in an important essay on spoken language, claims:

[5] David Bergamini, *The Universe* (Time-Life Books).

> The European middle-class culture is itself in chaos, its confidence long since lost and its capacity to find 'easy and full speech' evaporated . . . The language expressive of a competitive and mutually alienating society adopts a more and more minatory or defensive posture: fear of self exposure, fear of giving anything away means that the educated voice is developed as a means of concealment, not communication. The rich colour of the vernacular palate is reduced to a safe but drab, grey; rhythmic and grammatic subtleties are forced into a 'correct' strait jacket; even the mouth is forbidden to move.[6]

The danger of an abstract language is that it makes the general more important than the concrete, the impersonal theory more important than the personal experience. An abstract language makes our own life remote and elevates an abstract humanity which can be neither loved nor hated, simply because it does not exist. As Kierkegaard pointed out, such abstractions rob life of its rhythm and substance and, reducing everything to the same level, create a bloodless indolence.[7] The present trend towards the social sciences with their ready-made set of interlocking abstractions is indeed a depressing sign. Poetry, which is concerned with the unique celebration and understanding of the particular, has been, for the most part discarded. Where it exists it crouches like a frail flower below mountains of prose — as Charles Tomlinson says in a poem in which he imagines himself reading with Yevtushenko and Voznesensky:

> The reds return to their homeground stadia
> their unforeseen disgraces; I
> to the sobriety of a dawn-cold bed, to own
> my pariah's privilege, my three-inch spaces,
> the reader's rest and editor's colophon.[8]

The only poetry, the only symbolism we share is that which celebrates, makes divine, consumer trivia. Here anything,

---

[6] Charles Parker's essay, 'Culture, Education and the Deprived' in *Teachers for Tomorrow* (Heinemann Educational Books). *New Society* provides each week examples of the sort of abstract mechanically interlocking language I am describing. Here are two examples from a recent book, *The Death of the Family* by David Cooper (Allen Lane, The Penguin Press):

'The family as it is socially metamorphosed anonymises people'.

'The family is expert at the self-terrified and self-terrorizing inculcation of the non-necessity of entertaining doubts . . .'

[7] See Kierkegaard, *The Present Age* (Fontana Paperback).

[8] Charles Tomlinson, *Way of the World* (Oxford University Press).

providing it draws cash, is acceptable: a model of a burning monk can be constructed to evoke the need for ventilation; a reproduction of a Botticelli can be displayed to sell 'packaged tours' while the beautiful nakedness of woman can be used to sell anything. All that the consumer society touches it debases. Everywhere, life has been reduced to the tawdry and abstract arithmetic of the till.

What effects did the industrial and scientific revolution have on education, on the style and methods of education? The general rejection of imagination instituted in the schools, firstly the tyranny of facts (which lasted in this country up to the early fifties), and secondly, the tyranny of techniques (which we are becoming increasingly aware of in our schools and which further confirms our shift towards technocracy).

According to Gilbert Highet in his book *The Art of Teaching:*

> There was more poor teaching, there were more bad and hateful teachers (in the nineteenth century) than at any time since the middle ages . . . bad teachers rapidly multiplied and almost wrecked several important subjects by teaching them repulsively.

Highet provides three reasons to account for the situation: the accepted use of flogging and brutality as methods of discipline; the notion that education consisted of the systematic amassing of facts; the assumption that science provided a model on which every activity could be based. In short, due to a strange mixture of science and puritanism, education became mechanical and repressive.[9] Dickens in the opening chapters of *Hard Times* gives a grim portrait of the system. Mr M'Choakumchild has just completed his teacher training:

> He and some one hundred and forty other schoolmasters, had been lately turned at the same time, in the same factory, on the same principles, like so many pianoforte legs. He had been put through an immense variety of paces, and had answered volumes of head-breaking questions. Orthography, etymology, syntax and prosody, biography, astronomy, geography, and general cosmography, the sciences of compound proportion, algebra, land surveying and levelling, vocal music, and drawing from models, were all at the ends of his ten chilled fingers.

[9] The strange mixture of science and puritanism is further confirmed by many nineteenth century autobiographies. See, for example, John Ruskin's *Praeterita,* Edmund Grosse's *Father and Son,* and John Stuart Mill's *Autobiography.*

This litter of facts was then, under the name of education, violently stuffed into the child while all that was personal, growing, tentative, subtle, was ripped out and cast to the winds. Thus education became the path to collective madness which, because it was so common, was called common-sense, realism (Gradgrind, Dickens tells us, is a 'man of realities') and sanity. Gilbert Highet relates the absurdity of the educational system to the absurdity of the economic system: if education was the rough and impersonal accumulating of facts, it was in preparation for an economy which saw nothing beyond the production of goods and the accumulation of capital.

Today, education is more diverse. Art, Drama, English, have managed to free themselves from the shackles of functionalism and even science itself, at least in the primary schools is often given an experimental base. At the same time, and in essential conflict with some of the new approaches, schools have been reorganized on lines of big business. The main arguments for the large comprehensive schools are conducted in terms of quantities, utilities and facilities and the arguments are grounded on the knowledge of experts who have studied the sociology of administration. When large schools have to erect a 'communications system' you can be sure that there has been a fundamental disintegration of community which no communications systems however fashionable, can possibly restore. Yet our faith in techniques and gadgets remains unshaken. At interviews, prospective headmasters are expected to possess, first and foremost, administrative powers, while actual headmasters are urged to attend American business style conferences in order to learn indirect ways of controlling their staff. Interestingly enough, the old staff-meeting—where every teacher in the school could be present and viewpoints publicly aired—is fast disappearing and a complex system of sub-meetings, coming down from the headmaster and returning to him, is taking its place.

Even heads of departments are now attending management conferences. Recently there was such a conference for Heads of English Departments in Bristol; lectures ranged absurdly from *Shakespeare* to *The Role of the Manager,* from *Children's Self Discovery in Writing* to *In-Basket Material.* Books showing how business techniques can be employed in schools are the order of the day and the studies of Sociology and Psychology have made such terms as *feedback, quantification, socialization* and *motivation,* seem essential to any serious discussion of education.

It is not surprising that a considerable number of people have come to regard education as a functional activity which will be complete as soon as schools are able to buy all the necessary equipment. What else can the fashionable metaphor 'feedback' convey but a mechanical and utilitarian image of learning? Alongside these recent preoccupations, and providing them with a hidden emotional charge is a growing obsession among teachers for respectability and status. Teachers, it is said, are professionals. They are like solicitors, dentists, engineers. They institute, through techniques assimilated during their training the prescribed kinds of learning. Wherever one looks, the emphasis on techniques, on organization, on status, is constant.

Sociologists and psychologists tend to rely passively on current practices in schools for their definition of education. Thus in a recent book on teaching, a Professor of Education remarks:

> The characteristic of the teacher as a professional person is that he uses knowledge to organize, encourage and assist certain generally approved kinds of learning through a system of formal education.[10]

Typically, there is no questioning of the approved kinds of learning nor is there speculation as to whether education *might* consist of more than learning, might, for example, involve the development of the whole person. What should be is defined by what is. And possibilities are narrowed down to approved practices.

In America the faith in techniques is so complete that it has led, as it logically must, to a preference for relationships with machines:

> It is interesting to note then in many schools in the United States, children have developed an intense respect and affection for their computer teacher. The voice of the computer has been chosen for its warmth, friendliness, clarity and pleasantness. Thus the computer is always friendly . . . It is always fair: never plays favourites. It greets each student with a friendly 'Good morning, Johnny' (it always uses the student's name), and ends with an equally friendly, 'See you again on Monday, Johnny'.[11]

When machines are elevated to the level of persons, when friendships with machines are urged forward in the schools, and machines regulate the nature of the friendship, we have arrived at the furthest edge of technocracy. It is commonly declared that

[10] *Teaching the Teachers*, Edited by F. H. Hilliard (George Allen & Unwin).
[11] Herman Kahn, *The Times*, 9 October 1969.

Britain is five years 'behind' American 'progress', five years before complete insanity.

The Romantic movement from Blake, Coleridge, and Wordsworth to Shelley and Keats, to Ruskin, Morris and Carlyle, to Lawrence and Yeats does not only provide us with a remarkably articulate resistance to the destructive energies of industrial society, it also provides us with the means, not of securing yet another *system,* but of discovering a different manner of consciousness, a qualitative and symbolic mode of perception and understanding. Essentially the change would involve a partial return to an earlier and mythopoeic response. Brought into politics — I do not mean conventional party politics because all parties ride the same back of materialism — brought into *action* it would not necessarily entail the destruction of the technical achievements of our mechanical civilization, but it would involve a severe limiting of the artificial demands for greater consumption and production, for 'economic growth'. Ironically, it is the ceaseless demand for growth, for *over-*production and *over*-consumption which is largely responsible for destroying the quality of individual and social life today. Brought into politics, the Romantic movement would call a moratorium for the last quarter of the twentieth century — a time in which people could explore the possibilities of a different style of life, a style grounded in human activity, in making what is needed, in creating what is whole, in designing what is beautiful, and in rediscovering an experience of community which has been withheld from them by capitalist and state enterprise alike.

In an age riddled with misunderstandings — often engendered by the industry called 'communications' — it is perhaps necessary to state categorically that this is not to call for indulgence, for what journalists vaguely call 'permissiveness'. 'Permissiveness' is the counter-creation of a society based on compulsion: in order to produce we are compelled to a lifeless routine of work, then in our 'leisure' time, we are asked to 'get kicks', 'kill time' in order to consume, to passively sample the great supermarkets of packaged entertainments. As the degrading habit of clocking in is connected with the need for production, so 'permissiveness' is connected with the corresponding need for consumption. Our lives are the frailest shadows of the substance they could be.

What is required is an inward and imaginative discipline — a discipline which has been the possession of our major artists and creators. Creation is not rooted in the shallow soil of passive happiness, but in aspiration, in effort. Above all, it relishes that

sense of simultaneous stress and excitement which accompanies
any genuinely creative act. Such an imaginative discipline, unlike
current modish philosophies sees freedom not as an end but as a
condition *for* work, creation and community. I want to conclude
positively by indicating some of the qualities which distinguish the
poetic consciousness from the narrowly analytic. The word poetic
derives from the Greek *poieein* meaning to make, to create, to
synthesize. What sort of making is involved? What state of
consciousness does it need and nuture?.

In education, as in everyday life, we have generally assumed
that truth is something given, something securely anchored in the
solid bed of the material universe, which can be located, analysed
and duly hauled up for practical advantages. Truth for us has
been synonymous with knowledge, *useful* knowledge. Today the
educated man is considered to be the man who knows, the pedant
and more especially, the expert. Yet the Romantic movement
affirms that there are truths beyond the external world and the
powers of measurement, which are inseparable from the personal
and creative consciousness. As a result of the impact of science
and technology, we envisage education as a rail journey which
has a precise place and time for starting, continuing and arriving.
The arrival at the terminus is the purpose and end of the
travelling. The Romantic movement would have us regard
education more in the manner of the zigzag flight of the swift,
which does not move straight forward towards its object, which
enjoys its own movements and plays on the currents of the air.
Coleridge wanted to change the word knowledge into *grow*ledge:
but a noun inevitably suggests an object and to suggest an activity,
we need the verb, growing. Education, thus is a constant
unfurling, a reaching out and into, a becoming. We need to
substitute our mechanical and external logic for an inward and
poetic logic of consciousness, a logic developed to the point of
beauty in traditional Eastern civilization.

If the emphasis must change in the direction of the inward, so it
must also move away, though never completely, from content to
style. This means that we are not so much concerned with the
actual body of belief but more in the way in which is is held. Is it
alive? Honest? Courageous? Sensitive? Passionate? Keats, in a
letter, describes this certainty of style, this uncertainty in
knowledge:

> Though I myself am pursuing the same instinctive course as the
> veriest human animal you can think of . . . writing at

random—straining at particles of light in the midst of great darkness—without knowing the bearing of any one assertion of any one opinion, yet may I not in this be free from sin. May there not be superior beings amused with any graceful, though instinctive attitude my mind may fall into, as I am entertained with the alertness of a stoat or the anxiety of a Deer.[12]

The final outcome is unknown: one is immersed in the creating—but the poise of the mind *is* known, is experienced as a delight, valuable in itself. Van Gogh in a letter to Theo gives a similar testimony:

> Mauve takes offence at my having said 'I am an artist'—which I do not take back because that word included, of course, the meaning: 'I am seeking, I am striving, I am in with all my heart'. It is just the contrary from saying 'I know it, I have found it'.[13]

The search, and the qualities of being which the search calls for, becomes, to a large degree, its own justification. How different this is from our educated man, who knows but has no feelings, no sense of wonder or anguish towards that which he knows, who is a passive spectator, who, without any experience of contradiction can split his personal life from his public life, his being from his doing. And how different it is from the attitudes we instill in education. As teachers we habitually ask our children to sort out knowledge into two mechanical extremes expressed in such dichotomies as right/wrong, yes/no, either/or, true/false. We are responsible for destroying that groping experiential world between extremes, that 'graceful, instinctive' attitude which precedes knowledge and which alone gives 'answers' any depth of meaning.

Van Gogh's letter to his brother insists that his whole being is engaged in the act of creating. And this is a further quality of consciousness which the Romantic movement stressed. For the Romantic, an educated man is a man who is capable of simultaneously unifying reason, passion, and imagination and allows them to flow within, a dense but rapid stream. Yeats, to distinguish between the isolated abstract reason and the living psyche turned to two portraits which he describes in 'The Tragic Generation'. The first painting is of a Venetian gentleman by Strozzi. In this portrait Yeats discerns the living psyche:

[12] Letter of John Keats to George and Georgiana Keats, 19 March 1819.
[13] *Letters of Van Gogh.* Edited by Irving Stone.

Whatever thought broods in the dark eyes of that Venetian gentleman, has drawn its life from his whole body: it feeds upon it as the flame feeds upon the candle — and should that thought be changed, his pose would change, his very cloak would rustle for his whole body thinks.

The second portrait is of President Wilson by Sargent. Yeats comments:

> President Wilson lives only in the eyes, which are steady and intent; the flesh about the mouth is dead, and the hands are dead, and the clothes suggest no movement of his body, nor any movement but that of the valet, who has brushed and folded in mechanical routine. There (in the Venetian portrait) all was an energy flowing outward from the nature itself; here, all is the anxious study and slight deflection of external force.

President Wilson, with his thinking divorced from his passion, his mind from his body, looking out *at* the world could stand as a symbol of the man we today call a specialist, an authority, an expert, whereas the Venetian man, whose eyes express his being, his body, his vibrant wholeness is all that we should aspire to become.

Because we have split our own mind into irreconcilable levels, because we believe in exploration and research which leaves out the 'personal factor', we have come also to perceive the world in a similar way. We have come to regard Nature as little more than a complicated Meccano set which, being nothing more than a complex series of parts having no inherent order of its own, can be connected or disconnected as human will would have it. The creative consciousness however, affirms a different universe, vast, indivisible, with its own intrinsic rhythm and patterning. Coleridge claimed that his own education had prepared him to see such a universe:

> From my early reading of fairy tales and genii, my mind has been habituated to the vast.

> They (the Rationalists) contemplate nothing but *parts* and all parts are necessarily little. And the universe to them is but a mass of *little things* . . . I have known some who have been *rationally* educated, as it is styled. They were marked by a microscopic acuteness, but when they looked at great things, all became a blank and they saw nothing, and denied (very logically) that anything could be seen, and uniformly put the negation of a power for the possession of a power,

and called the want of imagination, judgement, and the never being
moved to rapture, philosophy![14]

Nature for us is matter for manipulation. We see it as a mass of
fragments, an endless series of hard surfaces. We redeem nature
by making her useful, by forcing her to serve Progress. In doing
this we are projecting our own divided consciousness on the
unknown face of the universe. The pollution of nature expresses
more than anything else the rank pollution of our own minds. To
perceive Nature differently, we need another mode of
consciousness, consciousness close to that suggested in Coleridge's
letter.

In the act of creation one finds oneself lapping against the
unknown. Keats claimed: 'My greatest elevations of soul leave me
every time more humbled'. It is the folly of our age to think that
everything can be explained, that everything is subject to laws
which, with the appropriate method, can be systematized through
the analytic reason. I would not wish to explain the inexplicable,
this apprehension of mystery which is an experience and not a
theoretical construct. But, perhaps, it can be best evoked by the
traditional paradox of the seed dying to live. 'I am most myself
when I transcend myself.' The self which is here transcended is
what Yeats called 'the mere daily self', the Self which is created, is
it the irreducible transcendent I? And yet, as I have argued in the
earlier part of this book, this experience depends on the act of
creation which in turn depends on a culture of artefacts, signs
and symbols.

Neither the eye, nor the mind can see itself unless reflected upon that
which it resembles.[15]

This insight is central. The mind cannot apprehend itself, rather
it discovers itself in those artefacts which it has inherited and
created and without which it would remain in utter helplessness
and darkness. Culture is the living transmission from one
generation to another, from one person to another, of symbols: of
poems, songs, myths, fables, stories, pictures, games, dances,
gestures, customs — without which the mind (implying here the
full play of consciousness, of which reason is only a part) cannot
realize, recognize and convey its own latent energies. It is this

[14] Coleridge, Letter to Thomas Poole, 16 October 1797.
[15] Shelley, 'A Defence of Poetry'.

culture which makes life worth living that we have all but lost. We need desperately to rediscover and recreate this culture and at all levels of society and in all types of activity, at work and at play, in the family and in the outside world.

In 'A defence of Poetry' Shelly claimed:

> The cultivation of poetry is never more to be desired than at periods when, from an excess of the selfish and calculating principle, the accumulation of the materials of external life, exceed the quantity of the power of assimilating them to the internal laws of human nature.

We live in a nervous age: a time of apocalypse, in which every day we witness a further extinction of individual qualities and achievements. About us is the pervasive feeling that civilization has disappeared completely, that only the force of inertia holds us together. There is no need to draw up the now familiar list of our violent and destructive acts. We need to ask 'What can we do?'. The cultivation of poetry in its broadest sense, the creation of symbols, the cultivation of style, the search for a numinous circumference: this is what is needed. And brought into action, into politics, it calls for an immediate moratorium, a suspension of all those technical and commercial activities falsely generated by an inhuman economy. It is, I know, an outrageous suggestion—insane by all modern criteria—but it is more than possible that anything which asks for less will not see us beyond the last quarter of our century and certainly not beyond the next.

Critics of this chapter may argue that my politics have become too poetic but I would see such criticism as being misconceived for it has been my intention to fuse poetry and politics. We must seek to make our lives as the poet seeks to make his poems, the potter his pots, the composer his symphonies. However, I do fear that the politics may remain not too poetic—for that is no fault—but too vague, too amorphous. I want, then, in my final essay to return to my theme, once again trying to make those vital connections between principle and practice lucid. In the attempt—it can be no more than that—I hope also to draw together the various premises on which these essays have been built.

NINE

Culture Against Civilization

> The machine appeared
> In the distance, singing to itself
> Of money. Its song was the web
> They were caught in, men and women
> Together. The villages were as flies
> To be sucked empty.
>   God secreted
> A tear. Enough, enough,
> He commanded, but the machine
> Looked at him and went on singing.

>   *R. S. Thomas*

As this book has constantly implied, we are living through a period of social and cultural disintegration. All the chants about progress and productivity, all the glittering images of publicity, all the bright slogans of advertising, do not, even though they distract the mind, conceal the truth. Any one whose work brings him into sensitive contact with people, whether he be a doctor, a psychotherapist, a teacher, a minister, a social worker, is aware of the storm of disturbance that now threatens the order and meaning of our society. A report, *Out of Mind*,[1] out at the moment of writing, reveals that nearly half of the beds in all our hospitals are taken by people suffering from some form of psychic disorientation. In many city schools we witness, as I have said, the stress, the *ennui* or violence that vitiates the experience of the young, who form in the telling phrase of the Albemarle Report 'the litmus paper of society'. There is a feeling of helplessness abroad, the feeling of events being out of control, of life not being lived. This feeling, while it may not be a direct response to popular scientific theories about man, is certainly supported and extended by current reductive notions which view life as 'nothing but' the product of the interaction between chance and necessity. With his freedom man loses his dignity and

---

[1] David Ennals, *Out of Mind* (ArrowBooks).

intentionality; unable to will his future, he drifts ever closer to the edge of nothingness.

All these signs and realities point to a complex condition of social collapse. Indeed they can be regarded as constituting what Arnold Toynbee in his *Study of History* sees as being the distinct pattern of a civilization in decline. It is, he writes, 'a common reaction of men who live out their lives in an age of social breakdown to ascribe their tribulations to the operations of an inexorable law of necessity or fate'. This feeling of being a piece of flotsam at the mercy of any and every current comes to be expressed in the dominant metropolitan culture. 'The soul surrenders itself to the melting pot and a negative sense of cultural promiscuity then comes to pervade every sphere of social activity.' In such an amorphous and destructive atmosphere, any ideal which gently or vehemently tugs man through time towards itself becomes not only problematic but also difficult to envisage. Culture, more and more in the hands of commercial and bureaucratic agencies, becomes amorphous and hedonistic: it deteriorates, indeed *has* visibly deteriorated in the last few years, to a 'leisure pursuit', a delicious or shocking sensation, a clever game, a distraction.

Yet, at the same time, a period of disintegration can release true creativity among those who passionately experience themselves as being spiritually unhoused within their own society. A minority of responsive individuals, sick unto death of what is about it, is able to leap beyond the confining pressures of the instant moment by projecting from the imagination a true commonwealth of the human spirit. It is this power to project a vision of society which holds out hope, however slender, for man in a period of social dissolution. Those who possess this power or seriously seek it form, in Toynbee's phrase, 'the internal proletariat'. One becomes a member of the internal proletariat as soon as one perceives the organized senselessness of industrial civilization and desires an alternative. It is not, as in the Marxist version of the proletariat, a question of mechanics but rather a question of individual consciousness. It is not a question of collectivities conflicting within an inevitable historical process but a question of individuals confronting existential decisions.

Who forms the internal proletariat in our society? Where is the minority, who may yet hold the key to the future, to be found? Without doubt it is a scattered proletariat: members of it are divided one from another. Yet occasionally it takes on shape and

articular purpose. The Welsh Language Society, the Movement
for Intermediate Technology, embody in different ways a
coherent search among the few for alternatives to hedonistic
technocracy. I believe that many of those who belong, knowingly
or not, to the internal proletariat are teachers of the arts and
creative humanities. The reasons for this are not hard to come by.
Perhaps the deepest reason resides in the fact that teachers of the
subjective disciplines are, as we have seen, pre-eminently
concerned with man *the animal symbolicum*. Yet it is precisely
this fundamental power of man, his power to shape and symbolize
the world which is most threatened by our society — for industrial
civilization has little room and no respect for the deep symbolic
needs of mankind. Like William Blake before him, William
Morris saw this clearly when he wrote at the end of the nineteenth
century:

> The world of modern civilization in its haste to gain a very
> inequitably divided material prosperity has entirely suppressed
> popular art.[2]

Or again,

> The death of Art was too high a price to pay for the material
> prosperity of the middle classes.[3]

In the place of true popular art, which both draws communities
together and enhances individual identities, we have now, for the
most part, a pseudo culture, manufactured in metropolitan
centres and unashamedly spewed out through the journalistic
media across the provinces. The art we hear about through the
media seldom embodies a specific experience in a specific place
in a specific sequence of time, it mostly conveys what is literal in
spirit, international in reference and commercial in origin.
Consider, for example, the import of the following extract, taken
from an article on contemporary art printed in *The Times* (that
bastion of technocratic capitalism and hence of art as big
business):

> You need a large group of young millionaires to really get a market in
> contemporary art moving . . . the market in contemporary art is
> essentially a fashionable affair . . . the bandwagon of contemporary
> sales has been gathering momentum in Paris.

[2] See *The Political Writings of William Morris* (Lawrence and Wishart).
[3] ibid.

Art as a consumer item—with high profits at stake. Just as we now have convenience food delivered in large quantities to big population centres debasing and mechanizing our eating and cooking habits, so we now have convenience culture, skilfully packaged for metropolitan taste, rapidly infecting our consciousness and jeopardizing our powers of creativity, our individuality.

It is in his opposition to convenience culture, from pop music to pop painting, from *The Sun* to the arts pages in *The Guardian* that the teacher of the subjective disciplines finds himself a member of that dissenting minority, the internal proletariat. He knows that a society in which the spirit of true art has been destroyed cannot survive long. He knows from the best of his work in the classroom and the seminar, as he does also from his knowledge of the past, that a true culture is an expression of a people with a distinct manner of life. He is, thus, from his experience, able to project into the future an ideal, a vision of a human commonwealth which transcends the calculated and insulting banality of contemporary artefacts. He may, also, have a shrewd suspicion that the school could be used to play an important part in the seemingly impossible task of transforming the conditions of modern society. Could not the place where he works become a new centre of gravity? The question brings us directly to a consideration of the politics of education.

What should be the contents of such a politics? I would like to begin to tackle the question by returning to the working premise of the creative teacher, to the notion, that is, that man is essentially a creator, an artist, a maker of symbols. David Jones in *Epoch and Artist* defined this premise with remarkable vigour:

> Art is the distinguishing dignity of man and it is by art that he becomes dignified and 'democracy' means nothing, or means something only bad, if it misconceives the right of man to exercise his distinctive function as man, i.e. as artist—as culture-making animal.

With this informing principle at the front of our minds, we can make the vague question of a general politics more specific by asking: *What are those conditions which most favour the development of culture?* If we can begin to answer this question we may be able to unravel the threads of a politics based on cultural principles.

To attempt an answer to the question I would suggest that, at least, the following conditions would seem to be essential for the full flowering of culture.

1. Conditions which are comparatively small scale.

2. Conditions in which trust rather than anxiety prevails.

3. Conditions in which people are held together by beliefs or values that transcend the everyday self.

It is essential that I now elaborate on each of these conditions.

It is commonly held in the West that there is a parallel development between culture (man's discovery and development of feeling and meaning through symbolism) and civilization (man's development of techniques by which he manipulates and organizes the external world). The study of history would seem to reveal that this is an unjustified assumption: a little introspection would reveal it to be little more than an arrogant illusion. From our own experience of technological expansion we know that, often, culture is destroyed by material advance. In an age of unfettered external advance it would seem that values, meanings, beliefs, psychic orientations are thrown into turmoil while anxiety gnaws the taproot of life. The most advanced countries have the most advanced figures for suicide, for alcoholism, for vandalism. Spengler, the historian, claimed that civilization-man and culture-man constituted antithetical modes of being: 'the energy of culture-man is turned inwards', he wrote, 'that of civilization-man outwards'. Such a formulation, I believe, overstates the dichotomy I wish to draw attention to, but it does embody an important aspect of the truth we are encouraged to ignore. *The conditions that most favour culture are not those which favour pure civilization.*[4]

Herbert Read pointed his finger towards the truth when he wrote:

> Culture is somehow related to smallness and minuteness. The greatest achievements in architecture, painting and literature are linked with relatively very small communities, city states like Athens, Florence, Siena . . . If we reverse the statement we can say without fear of contradiction that there is no historical evidence which in any way links the quality of culture with the magnitude of states . . . Quality is associated with limitations of size.[5]

It is in the intimate and rooted community that true art and discourse find those conditions in which it is possible for them to

---

[4] Mark Twain described civilization as 'a limitless multiplication of unnecessary necessaries'. This is what civilization without the proper human restraints imposed by true culture has become. Ideally civilization (concerned with technical development) and culture (concerned with the expression of feeling and meaning) should form complimentary concepts.

[5] Herbert Read, *The Grass Roots of Art* (Faber & Faber).

flourish. In the domain of education this was true for Plato's academy, for the early monasteries, and for our best schools and university departments today. Conversely is it because our vast comprehensive schools and faceless polytechnics defy this principle that they are bound to form deserts of the intellect and imagination. We tend to link small with provincial and provincial with dull partly because the provinces have been sucked dry by the cities and partly because we have been brain-washed to see it in that way.

Culture, also, develops most fully, I suggested, where love and trust prevail. This can be seen by considering the family where the power to symbolize experience originates in the enfolding love between the mother and the child. D. W. Winnicott in *Playing and Reality* claimed:

> The potential space (where play and culture develop) between baby and mother, between child and family, between individual and society or the world, depends on experience which leads to trust. It can be looked upon as sacred to the individual in that it is here that the individual experiences creative living. By contrast, exploitation of this area leads to a pathological condition.

There is good reason to suppose that the problems we face in our society derive, in large measure, from a failure in nurture: a failure, that is, to develop in our domestic lives, rites and rituals, games and phantasies, and all those many languages and ceremonies through which we are able to meet and absorb experience. As in the opening chapter I have developed the positive side of Winnicott's argument, I would like here to confine my remarks to the way in which the exploitation of culture may lead to a pathological reality. At the moment the family, which is being severely eroded by the pressures of the media, seems to possess few periods of sustained time in which relationships can unfold and events be experienced and assimilated. The child instead of playing and symbolizing in relationship to his needs and family experiences is encouraged to adopt mechanical substitutes. As we saw in Chapter 4 the media has been quick to realize that today's babies form tomorrow's market.

In brief, inside the family itself, a synthetic culture based on the need to create anxiety, to foster clichés, to bully and bamboozle has developed with extraordinary success and with alarming consequences. It is becoming clear that more and more young people, being deprived of a genuine heritage, are deprived at the same time of the means of achieving an identity.

Furthermore, the endless manufacturing of images and symbols, designed to deceive and exploit, not only menaces the development of the young in our society, it also confounds that trust which is an essential element of true symbolization. Culture becomes a branch of publicity; the organic comes to be regarded as an undeveloped form of the synthetic and even trust is seen as a subtle form of deception. Where are the experiences in our society which lead to trust and make possible creative living?

The third condition for the flowering of culture, that of possessing values or beliefs which transcend the self I have elaborated in the previous chapter. It must suffice to say here that in the act of creating we invariably find ourselves reaching out, arching over a curve of time which takes us towards what we only, at the point of creating, dimly apprehend. To create is to risk, to leap out of the mundane self in an effort to transform and transcend. It would seem axiomatic that man only creates when he believes that creating has a value beyond 'reflexes', 'mechanisms' and 'releases'. If we really believed that we were nothing but a complex biochemical mechanism we would lose our passion to explore, symbolize and share our experience.

From these three premises we may begin tentatively to draw up a politics of education, having both a critical and a creative function.

If we believe that the small scale is vital, we must oppose the tendency to centralize, to draw all the diverse forms of production and activity into fewer and larger units. We must assert that large invariably means worse because it destroys the cultural and social diversity and replaces it with uniformity. We need to proclaim a positive policy of decentralization. As Dr E. F. Schumacher asserts, 'Small is Beautiful'.[6]

If we believe that culture to thrive needs not only the small scale but also conditions which are free from exploitation and anxiety, we must energetically oppose all those forms of manufactured culture which cheapen and debase. We must criticize and oppose the methods of advertising, the methods of the gutter-press, the synthetic mass production of pop music, of teenage magazines, of pornography and, we must be prepared to point out the sharp decline of the quality papers into intellectual slickness, into fashion, cleverness and gossip.

---

[6] This is the title of a book by the economist E. F. Schumacher published by Blond Briggs. Readers interested in the philosophy of the small-scale society should also refer to Leopold Kohr's *The Breakdown of Nations* (Christopher Davies).

Instead of closing schools, as the de-schoolers would have us do, we must endeavour to transform them into political and cultural centres both serving their own communities and the essential needs of the imagination and the intellect.

Finally, I suggest we should conceive our politics within the broad categories of civilization and culture. 'Civilizations', according to Oswald Spengler, 'are the most external and artificial states of which a species of developed humanity is capable.' There are many now who would like to see schools serve the artificial society by preparing children for the rows of desks in typing pools and non-stop assembly lines. As the artificial environment spreads out its long mechanical tentacles, so it draws more and more of the energies of man into itself. In advanced civilization human life crowds into a few giant world cities. All around these densely populated cities, where life has lost all contact with the rhythms of the seasons and of the earth, lie, except for a few farming industries and leisure centres, ribbed by monotonous motorways, the drained and empty provinces. This is a process that must be reversed if life is to retain meaning and quality. Life must be freed from the petrified world cities.

Such a transformation is daunting. It will not happen easily or quickly. But teachers could make a beginning by developing radically new uses for their schools and by making society more aware of the momentous issues that now challenge humanity. I have argued that many teachers feel they guard values and potentialities which technocracy fatally ignores or dismisses. For this reason many teachers are members of that internal proletariat who in the chaos of the present look forward to that varied and cultured commonwealth which must embody the only sane hope for the future. As Arnold Toynbee says:

> Those who neither acquiesce in the disintegration of their society nor seek to hold back the tide with artificial substitutes for creativity, but who have the vision and the courage to confront the challenge, have it within their reach to participate in a greater sort of creation than is witnessed in even the most vigorous stages of social growth.[7]

---

[7] Arnold Toynbee, *A Study of History* (Oxford).

Short Bibliography

Books on Anthropology, Psychology, Philosophy and Aesthetics (relating to Sections 1 and 3).

ANTHROPOLOGY

Ernst Cassirer: *An Essay on Man*, (Bantam Books).

Stanley Diamond: *In Search of the Primitive* (Transaction Books, USA).

Susanne Langer: *Philosophy in a New Key*, (Mentor Books).

Lewis Mumford: *The Pentagon of Power*, (Secker and Warburg).

Michael Polanyi: *Personal Knowledge*, (Routledge & Kegan Paul).

Herbert Read: *Ikon and Idea*, (Faber & Faber).

Theodore Roszak: *Where the Wasteland Ends*, (Faber & Faber).

Oswald Spengler: *The Decline of the West*, (Alfred Knopf).

Arnold Toynbee: *A Study of History*, (Oxford).

PSYCHOLOGICAL

Erik Erikson: *Childhood and Society*, (Penguin).

Victor Frankl: *Psychotherapy and Existentialism*, (Penguin).

David Holbrook: *Human Hope and the Death Instinct*, (Pergamon).

Marjorie Hourd: *Relationship in Learning*, (Heinemann Educational Books).

Liam Hudson: *The Cult of the Fact*, (Jonathan Cape).

Carl Jung: *The Undiscovered Self*, (Routledge & Kegan Paul).

R. D. Laing: *The Divided Self*, (Penguin).

Rollo May: *Love and Will*, (Souvenir Press).

D. W. Winnicot: *Playing and Reality*, (Tavistock).

AESTHETIC

R. Arnheim: *Towards a Psychology of Art*, (Faber & Faber).

Matthew Arnold: *Culture and Anarchy*.

G. H. Bantock: *Education, Culture and the Emotions*, (Faber & Faber).

T. S. Eliot: *Notes Towards a Definition of Culture*, (Faber & Faber).

David Jones: *Epoch and Artist*, (Faber & Faber).

F. R. Leavis: *Nor Shall My Sword*, (Chatto & Windus).

Marion Milner: *On Not Being Able to Paint*, (Heinemann Educational Books).

William Morris: *Political Writings*

Herbert Read: *Education Through Art*, (Faber & Faber).

Friedrich Schiller: *On the Aesthetic Education of Man*, (Oxford).

Percy Shelley: *An Essay on Poetry*

Christopher Small: *Ariel like a Harpy*, (Gollancz).

PHILOSOPHICAL

Peter Abbs (Editor): *The Challenge of Existantialism*, (*Tract 17*, Gryphon Press).

William Barret: *Irrational Man*, (Heinemann Educational Books).

Martin Buber: *Between Man and Man*, (Fontana).

Marjorie Grene: *The Knower and the Known*, (Faber & Faber).

John MacMurray: *The Self as Agent*, (Faber & Faber).

Roubiczek: *Existentialism*, (Cambridge University Press).

Werner Pelz: *The Scope of Understanding in Sociology*, (Routledge & Kegan Paul).

Roger Poole: *Towards Deep Subjectivity*, (Allen Lane/The Penguin Press).

2. Books on Imaginative Writing (relating to Chapter 3).

Peter Abbs: *English for Diversity*, (Heinemann Educational Books).

A. B. Clegg: *The Excitement of Writing*, (Chatto & Windus).

Patrick Creber: *Sense and Sensitivity*, (University of London Press).

Robert Druce: *The Eye of Innocence* (University of London Press).

David Holbrook: *English in Australia* now *English for the*

Rejected, (Cambridge University Press).

Marjorie Hourd: *The Education of the poetic Spirit*, (Heinemann Educational Books).

—*On Creative Thinking*, (Tract 13: Gryphon Press).

—*Coming into their Own*, (Heinemann Educational Books).

Ted Hughes: *Poetry in the Making*, (Faber & Faber).

Margaret Langdon: *Intensive Writing*

Sybil Marshall: *An Experiment in Education* (Cambridge University Press).

Dorothy Owen: *The Child Vision*, (Manchester University Press, 1920).

Marie Peel: *Seeing to the Heart*, (Chatto & Windus).

Denys Thompson: *Children as Poets*, (Heinemann Educational Books).

3. Books on Advertising, the Mass-media and the English-teacher (relating to Chapter 4).

Peter Abbs (Editor): *The Black Rainbow,* (Heinemann Educational Books).

—*The Politics of Education*, (Gryphon Press).

John Berger: *Ways of Seeing*, (Penguin).

Seymour Betsky: *Towards a Critique of Industrial Culture* (*Tract 16*, Gryphon Press).

Daniel Boorstin: *The Image*, (Penguin).

Ron Goulart: *The Assault on Childhood*, (Gollancz).

S. I. Hayakawa: *Language in Thought and Action*, (Allen & Unwin).

Jules Henry: *Culture against Man*, (Penguin).

Richard Hoggart: *The Use of Literacy*, (Penguin).

David Holbrook: *The Masks of Hate*, (Pergamon).

Fred Inglis: *The Imagery of Power*, (Heinemann Educational Books).

Vance Packard: *The Waste-Makers*, (Penguin).

Ian Robinson: *The Survival of English*, (Cambridge University Press).

Denys Thompson (Editor): *Discrimination and Popular Culture,* (Heinemann Educational Books).

Raymond Williams: *Communications*, (Penguin).

Index